Poetry: Big Thoughts in Small Packages

Lucy Calkins, Stephanie Parsons, and
Amy Ludwig VanDerwater

Photography by Peter Cunningham

HEINEMANN ◆ PORTSMOUTH, NH

This book is dedicated to Lee Bennett Hopkins—with gratitude for your poems, your wisdom, and your generosity

Heinemann
361 Hanover Street
Portsmouth, NH 03801–3912
www.heinemann.com

Offices and agents throughout the world

The authors and publisher wish to thank those who have generously given permission to reprint borrowed material:

"Why Poetry?" Copyright © 1966 by Lee Bennett Hopkins. First appeared in *Bee Cullinan's House of Poetry: Ideas and Activities Across the Curriculum that You Can Use to Bring Poetry into Your Classroom*, published by Boyds Mill Press. Reprinted by permission of Curtis Brown, Ltd.

"Pencil Sharpener," "Ceiling," "Inside My Heart," by Zoë Ryder White. Courtesy of Zoë Ryder White.

"Aquarium," by Valerie Worth. From *All the Small Poems and Fourteen More* © 1994 by Valerie Worth. Reprinted by permission of Farrar, Straus, and Giroux, LLC. All rights Reserved.

"Between Two Trees," "Lullaby," "Fly Fishing in Crystal River," and "Destiny" from *Old Elm Speaks: Tree Poems* by Kristine O'Connell George. Text copyright © 1998 by Kristine O'Connell George. Reprinted by permission of Clarion Books, an imprint of Houghton Mifflin Harcourt Publishing Company. All rights reserved.

"Owl Moon Haiku," by Jane Yolen. Copyright © 2013 by Jane Yolen. Reprinted by permission of Curtis Brown, Ltd.

Excerpt from "Valentine for Ernest Mann," by Naomi Shihab Nye from *Red Suitcase*. Copyright © 1994 by Naomi Shihab Nye. Reprinted with the permission of The Permissions Company, Inc., on behalf of BOA Editions, Ltd. www.boaeditions.org.

"Go Wind," by Lilian Moore from *I Feel the Same Way* by Lilian Moore.

Copyright © 1967 by Lilian Moore. All Rights Reserved. Used by permission of Marian Reiner.

"Way Down in the Music," by Eloise Greenfield from *Honey, I Love and Other Love Poems* by Eloise Greenfield. Text copyright © 1978 by Eloise Greenfield. Used by permission of HarperCollins Publishers and the author.

"Poem [2]" from *The Collected Poems of Langston Hughes* by Langston Hughes, edited by Arnold Rampersad with David Roessel, Associate Editor, copyright © 1994 by the Estate of Langston Hughes. Used by permission of Alfred A. Knopf, a division of Random House, Inc. Any third party use of this material, outside of this publication, is prohibited. Interested parties must apply directly to Random House for permission. Also reprinted by permission of Harold Ober Incorporated.

Excerpt from "Everything Is a Poem," from *Everything Is a Poem: The Selected Best of J. Patrick Lewis*. Reprinted by permission of J. Patrick Lewis.

"Robin" and "Waiting Room Fish," by Amy Ludwig VanDerwater. Copyright © 2012 by Amy Ludwig VanDerwater. First appeared on author's blog, the Poem Farm Blog. Reprinted by permission of Curtis Brown, Ltd.

"Maples in October," by Amy Ludwig VanDerwater. Copyright © 2013 by Amy Ludwig VanDerwater. First appeared in *Forest Has a Song*, published by Clarion Books. Reprinted by permission of Curtis Brown, Ltd.

Cataloging-in-Publication data is on file with the Library of Congress.

ISBN-13: 978-0-325-04731-7

Production: Elizabeth Valway, David Stirling, and Abigail Heim
Cover and interior designs: Jenny Jensen Greenleaf
Series includes photographs by Peter Cunningham, Nadine Baldasare, and Elizabeth Dunford
Composition: Publishers' Design and Production Services, Inc.
Manufacturing: Steve Bernier

Printed in the United States of America on acid-free paper
21 20 19 18 17 VP 2 3 4 5 6

Acknowledgments

POET PABLO NERUDA knew that poetry sprouts from peoples' lives: "I grew up in this town, my poetry was born between the hill and the river, it took its voice from the rain, and like the timber, it steeped itself in the forests." A book like this comes from our lives too, and we feel grateful to many people for their wisdom and influence and hard work as we journeyed these hills together.

Poetry has been a big part of the Teachers College Reading and Writing Project since the organization began, more than thirty years ago. Georgia Heard was one of the first two staff developers at the Project, and her trail-blazing book, *For the Good of the Earth and the Sun,* became part of the firmament in the Project. Katie Wood Ray joined the Project's staff a few years after Georgia left, and she carried the torch for poetry, passing it onto Nick Flynn and Shirley McPhillips, who wrote yet another gorgeous book on poetry, *A Note Slipped Under the Door.* More recently it is Audra Robb who takes the lead role, carrying the torch for poetry. Audra has often graced our organization by giving poems as gifts, reading poems to mark occasions, and bringing poems into every part of the school year. We are grateful to all these people; they provide the context out of which this book emerges.

Of course, while there have always been staff developers at the Project who personify the organization's love of poetry, there have also been hero poets who come to us now and again and who leave us forever changed. Lucille Clifton spoke at a Saturday reunion when Los Angeles was burning up with the Rodney King riots. "Nurture your image of what's possible," she said to us. "You can't create what you can't imagine." Billy Collins and Nikki Giovanni have also spoken at Project institutes, and they, like Naomi Shihab Nye, Jim Howe, and Lee Bennett Hopkins, are heroes to us and to the children we teach. Several poets generously opened their notebooks to us, explaining how they find poems and how they tune these poems carefully. Thank you to J.

Patrick Lewis, Joyce Sidman, Jane Yolen, and Kristine O'Connell George for taking us behind the scenes of your poetry and writing lives.

We are blessed to work with an amazing publisher for professional books: Heinemann. Kate Montgomery, Abby Heim, and Teva Blair have led the effort to which this book belongs, and their vision and energy are an inspiration to us. Their deep understanding and knowledge of writing have strengthened the book. Zoe Ryder White was more than an editor. A poet herself, Zoe not only sanded and polished again and again, finding rough spots and making them smooth, but she also wrote alongside us. Some of Zoe's poems also live within the book.

We hadn't imagined that this book would be given such a total make-over. The original book, written almost a decade ago, was a great favorite of ours and of many readers, and so we imagined, for a time, that that original book would only need to be buffed and polished. Instead, we've done a total, head-to-toe rewrite. The effort required heroic amounts of work and was something we could pull off only because we had help from Hareem Khan, who wrote from Pakistan, working while we slept. Julia Mooney, co-author of *Lessons from the Masters,* helped by writing into this manuscript as well. We're grateful.

As you read these pages, listen for voices of young poets at work and play. These voices are real children's voices from across the United States, and we would like to tip our figurative hats to all of the teachers, children, and parents who have shared their joyful and honest poetry with us all.

The class described in this unit is a composite class, with children and partnerships of children gleaned from classrooms in very different contexts, then put together here. We wrote the units this way to bring you both a wide array of wonderful, quirky, various children and also to illustrate for you the predictable (and unpredictable) situations and responses this unit has created in classrooms across the nation and world.

—Lucy, Stephanie, and Amy

Contents

BEND III   Trying Structures on for Size

 Registration instructions to access the digital resources that accompany this book may be found on p. ix.

Welcome to the Unit

NOW THAT THE BOOKS ARE ALMOST DONE and we have been speaking to our readers, people have been asking lots of questions about the new series. Among those questions, we've heard is "Why a book on poetry?" Frankly, the question takes us by surprise. For us, it would be easier to imagine people asking, "Why isn't there a book on poetry at every grade?" because we wish that was the case. For that question, we have our answer ready, because the *If . . . Then . . . Curriculum* book does indeed detail the way a unit on poetry might go for every grade. But no, the question is "Why a book on poetry?" and the source of the question is the fact that poetry is not one of the three types of writing that has been highlighted in the world class standards. That is, when the standards suggests the school day should give equal time to the three types of writing, they are referring to opinion, information, and narrative writing, and poetry is not on the list.

We have a few answers. First, we actually believe that as a result of the creation of world-class standards, the emphasis on poetry will ultimately increase, not decrease. The standards will come to be defined by the way they are tested, and as far as we can detect, poetry will play an increasingly large role in new assessments because the push will be to engage students in more analytic reading of short complex texts. World-class standards ask that students can read, looking at the craft choices authors have made, and ask, "What does that choice have to do with the central meanings of this text?" Poetry is supremely suited to this sort of close, interpretive, analytic reading and can serve as a gateway to close reading of other kinds of texts as well. The standards, too, are clear that at a young age, children need to be able to identify literary devices and to discuss the effects of techniques such as alliteration and repetition on the flow and meaning of the overall text. By third grade, the world-class standards expect readers to refer in technical terms to parts of texts, including lines and stanzas in poetry. That is, we believe

there will be a premium placed on reading poetry, if not on writing poetry, in upcoming high-stakes assessments. And there is no better way to teach young readers an awareness of craft decisions and their relationship to authors' purposes—appreciation for the significance of where a poet has chosen to create line breaks or recognition of the insight that a poet achieves through creating a surprising metaphor—than to engage those readers in similar decisions as poetry writers. So yes, we do believe that poetry will be in the spotlight in the years to come.

We want to stress that decisions about what one teaches can't be outsourced. Ultimately, each one of us is the author of our own life, and that means, too, that we are each the author of our own teaching. We must always be able to say, "This is *my teaching*, by me." And to my colleagues and me at the Teachers College Reading and Writing Project, a language arts curriculum that includes no poetry would be unimaginable.

Poetry reminds us to slow down and read every word, every pause, to listen to what is said and how it is said. Poetry stretches us, requiring us to see how an old tree is like a grandmother. A study of poetry teaches children to explore ideas and language, valuing voice and metaphor and sensory detail. And because poetry is often short, this genre allows children to explore the intersection between language, structure, and meaning. Considering every part of a poem, including the spacing and shape of the words on the page, the type and size of the font, even the white space that surrounds the text as meaningful elements: this offers children multiple opportunities to make decisions based on meaning, reinforcing the crucial reading/writing/thinking concept that nothing we read or write is accidental, and therefore everything is worth interpreting.

And in truth, we feel fortunate to have written a book that teaches children to seek and cherish small observations, sewing them into finely crafted poems.

For poetry is greater than rhyme, greater than metaphor; poetry is connection. When we teach children to write poems, we teach them to organize their dreams, memories, wonderings, and favorite facts into folded treasures, treasures that will find homes in readers' minds and hearts. It is our hope that you and your students will find beauty and surprise on poetry's path and that what you learn will follow you into all other genres.

Second-graders sometimes become "quantity writers," believing that the more they write, the better it is. This unit, with its focus on clarity and precise language, will help children reread and listen to the sounds of their words. These habits transfer to other genres of reading and writing, partly because poetry itself spans other genres: there are informational poems, opinion poems, and narrative poems. We can look to this range of poetry to supplement our students' understanding of the craft work at the heart of poetry and prose. If we show students how Valerie Worth writes about a soap bubble and describes how it "Bends out of shape/On the air,/Leans, rounds again,/Rises, shivering, heavy," we can then invite our young writers to pay closer attention to their use of verbs, to try, as Worth does, to make each verb paint a precise picture. This poetic practice matters in any genre.

All year long, your students have been speaking in small poems. "I keep a stone in my pocket, smooth as a whisper." "My cat makes a circle on our chair. She looks like a furry orange cake!" New to the world, children speak with a freshness that adult poets work to grow in their own writing. This genre takes time to wrap its arms around these fresh and metaphorical ways of seeing the world. In this unit, you will help children find poetry in life, and then you will teach them techniques that add life into poetry.

OVERVIEW OF THE UNIT

This poetry unit is divided into three bends, each one deepening childrens' understandings of poetry. First, students will learn that poets are sparked by objects and feelings that they translate to music on the page. This early part of the unit, with its special attention to sound, will help develop students' ears as they experiment with line breaks, as they come to understand that a poem is different from a story. A poem looks different from prose, and line breaks help a reader know when to pause. As the unit progresses in Bend II, children will recognize that in a poem, choice and placement of words matter more than ever. They will admire and experiment with metaphor, strengthening their ability to see like poets. You will not focus on teaching rhyme or forms such as haiku or diamante, but rather on meaning and crafting through repetition, metaphor, white space, and language. As you round Bend III, children will explore various natural structures of poems: story poems, poems with a back-and-forth structure, list poems.

Bend I introduces students to the sounds and feelings of poetry by having them read poems aloud in groups, with partners, and alone. The brevity and music of poetry invites repeated readings, and by reading poems again and again, children will begin to internalize the varied rhythms of this genre. By spending early time with favorite poems, you will have many teachers as you write through the unit. This unit is peppered with poetry from many poets, especially Kristine O'Connell George, and you will want to collect favorite poems of your own. Each poem will silently offer your writers guidance as they choose topics, structures, metaphors, language, and line breaks for their poems. During these early days, children will explore objects and memories, recognizing the poetry in their own lives.

In this first bend, set up a table or corner where you will collect humble and beautiful objects from nature: small rocks, nests, shells, snakeskin sheds. The very first few days of this unit will focus on how poets see and hear the world differently and how children can and do see with "poets' eyes." Writer Annie Dillard said, "How we spend our days is, of course, how we spend our lives," and by collecting and studying natural objects, you will teach children that this is a worthy way to spend life—drawing, thinking, wondering, comparing. The work of poetry is not simply making marks on paper; it is work of deepening observation. These early days are for inner work, deep seeds that will later flower into leafy poems. You will help the children learn to listen and to see and to care. Children will write many poems about pine cones and dandelions, making comparisons and experimenting with line breaks. They will soon move to writing about their own topics, just as they have in all other units, learning that their own stories and wonderings can be shaped into poems too. You will teach them how poets choose topics that matter, topics that hold big feelings in moments or images. Your class will discover poems in their own lives and will discuss where favorite poets may have found their inspiration. Students will understand that spelling matters in poetry, recognizing that each word must be clear to readers. To this end, you will teach a new strategy for editing for spelling as students prepare for a first small poetry celebration.

In Bend II, your students will have even more opportunities to dive into work and play with language. The lessons in this bend focus on how poets choose precise words, use repetition, and convey feelings. Together, you will notice how poems have different moods and how poets choose words and rhythms to match these moods. Children will collect poems in their folders, annotating them to indicate places where poets did something interesting with words, and you will encourage them to use these collected poems as mentors, experimenting with these same techniques. Because they will be writing many poems, each lesson and technique you teach can be used to write a new poem or to revise an old favorite. This bend places a special emphasis on metaphor, first helping children to make comparisons and then teaching them to sustain one metaphor over several lines. As you teach new tools, you'll also remind poets to draw on their full repertoire of poetry strategies. Expect them to be able to tell you what they are trying out: "I used lots of repeating in my poem to show how dizzy I really felt."

Bend III will continue your study of all aspects of poetic language, but you will especially focus on structure, teaching students that poets choose structures. The lessons in this bend will help children "fly above" various poems, noticing particularly how they are sewn together. Your lessons will teach children to read like writers as they name how some poems are story poems, some are lists with twists, and some have a back-and-forth structure. Be prepared that your children will likely notice aspects of structure you have not introduced; children are very observant and interested in reading like writers. During this bend, you might choose to look at a one-poet collection, such as *Old Elm Speaks* by Kristine O'Connell George, noticing the many ways she approaches the topic of trees: story poems, list poems, mask poems. This bend will not focus on forms such as limerick and haiku, but rather, on more natural structures that we often find in poetry. Your class will play with point of view, realizing that they can pretend to speak to something or as something or create imaginary back-and-forth conversations in the shape of poems. This final bend will end as children revise their poems for careful language, edit, and celebrate their poems in a variety of ways.

ASSESSMENT

As with any unit, it will be important for you to know what knowledge and experience your students bring to this unit on writing poetry. Before the unit begins, you may decide to give students an on-demand writing assessment. You might say, "Writers, today I'm going to give you some time to write a poem about something that matters to you. Remember to use everything you know about good poetry writing." As you observe most students "finishing" their poems, you might ask them to take their revision pens and revise! This will show you what they know about revising poetry as well. You may decide to give them the whole thirty minutes of the workshop time, or just fifteen to twenty minutes on the first day, leaving more time for children to share their ideas and questions about poetry after they have written. Some questions that might drive your observation of student work might be What do students think poetry is? What do students remember about studying poetry from last year? What are students using from the units you have studied so far this year? Are students selecting meaningful topics? Do students write with details? How are students using line breaks, white space, and punctuation? You will also want to keep in mind the qualities of good writing that you use throughout every genre study: meaning, structure, elaboration, craft, and conventions.

After this initial assessment you will want to use the information you have gathered about your students to drive the instruction of the unit. Use the patterns you notice in student work to help you plan whole-class minilessons and small strategy groups.

In addition to the on-demand assessment you administer at the beginning of the unit, you can collect formative assessments of your students throughout the unit by looking through their writing folders and asking questions during conferences to assess growth. Some questions you might ask include:

- "Can you tell me about this topic?"

- "What do you hope readers see, think, or feel when they read this poem?"

- "How did you use your poets' eyes in this poem?"

- "What images are you planning to add for your readers?"

- "How will you use white space or line breaks in this poem?"

- "How are you paying attention to sound in this poem?"

- "Can you show me some very specific words you have chosen, and tell me why?"

- "I notice that you _____. How is that decision working in your poem?"

- "Are you trying to achieve something with this poem that is hard for you?"

- "How are you planning to revise?"

Children's answers to these questions can guide you in choosing what and how to teach them in conferences and small groups.

Be sure to give your students an opportunity at the end of the unit to do another on-demand poem as a summative assessment so that you can compare the two pieces of writing and see how students are using what they have learned. Consider both the qualities of good writing and your main goals of the unit to assess how kids grew as poets and writers.

GETTING READY

You will find some helpful resources in the online resources. You might want to print the bibliography of suggested poetry books and check what your library has available. Offer your children a variety of poetry books about a variety of topics. While everyone loves funny poems, it is important for students to see that poetry can touch all emotions. Like good friends, one poem might make readers laugh and one might make us cry. One poem might pause and celebrate beauty, and one might frolic with the sounds of words. When you choose books and mentor poems, be sure to choose many unrhymed poems, because this unit focuses on poetic techniques other than rhyme, strict meter, and form. Look for poems with great metaphors, interesting line breaks, repetition, alliteration, and clever points of view.

Take note, too, of the digital resources. There is a generous poetry community online, and you will find a handful of websites offering poems, minilessons, and poetry videos for the classroom. These can be projected on a screen, or you might offer children the opportunity to visit a poetry site when you are at the computer lab.

We recommend Kristine O'Connell George's *Old Elm Speaks* as a mentor text to carry you through this unit. All about trees, this book offers a variety of structures and viewpoints, a close attention to word choice, and a celebration of finding poetry in the every day. You will find a few poems from *Old Elm Speaks* in these pages, and you will likely want to add it to your classroom library.

For your lessons, you are welcome to print the pages of children's poems. Copy them onto classroom charts so that everyone can make observations about various techniques, or print them for your students, allowing them to recite poems together and even annotate them, marking what they notice about the topic or craft.

Look around your classroom. What in the room or outside your window might inspire you to write a poem? If you have thought much about this before, this is a perfect time to bring more beauty and intrigue into your room. Set up a small kaleidoscope or a clear bowl full of water and rocks. Hang a prism by the window or leave some unusual articles from the newspaper on the windowsill. By surrounding your children with what the world has to offer, you provide them with subjects for poems.

ONLINE DIGITAL RESOURCES

A variety of resources to accompany this and the other Grade 2 Units of Study in Opinion, Information, and Narrative Writing are available in the online resources. To access and download all the digital resources for this grade-level set:

1. Go to **www.heinemann.com** and click the link in the upper right to log in. (If you do not have an account yet, you will need to create one.)

2. **Enter the following registration code** in the box to register your product: **WUOS_GR2**

3. Enter the security information requested, obtained from within your unit book.

4. Once you have registered your product it will appear in the list of "View my registered Online Resources, Videos, and eBooks." (Note: You only need register once; then each time you return to your account, just click the "My Online Resources" link to access these materials.)

(You may keep copies of these resources on up to six of your own computers or devices. By downloading the files you acknowledge that they are for your individual or classroom use and that neither the resources nor the product code will be distributed or shared.)

Seeing with Poets' Eyes

IN THIS SESSION, you'll teach students that poets see the world through special lenses. They see with both their hearts and minds, and they write about the world in fresh, unusual ways.

GETTING READY

✔ You will want to arrange your room so that poems are featured prominently. You might have a basket of poetry books by your chair, poems displayed on the walls, and mentor poems you and your students will study together during this unit.

✔ A basket of treasures (scissors, shells, pebbles, pinecones, acorns, feathers, safety pins, and so on) that you'll have beside you for the minilesson and that you'll pull out for students to study with poets' eyes (see Connection, Teaching)

✔ A basket of similar objects for each table, chosen to teach youngsters to observe carefully (shells, driftwood, leaves, special rocks, and so on); you'll soon invite children to add their own objects to these collections (see Link).

✔ "Pencil Sharpener," "Ceiling," and other poems of your choice, enlarged on chart paper (see Teaching and Active Engagement)

✔ Special new poetry folders (or cleaned-out old folders) to mark this momentous occasion

✔ Paper with room for both pictures and words; you may also want to give each child a clipboard if you have enough.

✔ New chart titled "Reading Poetry Like a Poet (see Share)

✔ At some point before teaching Session 2's minilesson, read with your students the poem "Aquarium," by Valerie Worth (or another poem of your choice). "Aquarium" is highlighted in Session 2, so if you choose another poem, be sure your students are familiar with it before Session 2.

✔ One poetry folder for each child to collect copies of mentor poems; (if you are able to get permission to copy them; other options include creating a stapled booklet of mentor poems or posting mentor poems on a wall or bulletin board)

I F YOUR CLASSROOMS ARE LIKE OURS, the launch of the poetry unit will not be the first time students have been exposed to poetry. In fact, we imagine that you will have been reading them poems throughout the year, maybe especially so in the weeks leading up to this unit. We imagine that students have been encouraged to bring poems they love to school, that poems have been read to mark special occasions or make ordinary occasions special. Like any genre, reading poetry paves the way for writing it. So we imagine that you and your students have been looking forward to this day, the first day of the poetry unit, with great anticipation. Today your students will transition from being poetry enthusiasts to poetry writers, and you will help them begin to live and see as poets do, ready to catch poems out of the air.

> *"Today your students will transition from being poetry enthusiasts to poetry writers."*

Lee Bennett Hopkins, poet, author, and anthologist of over 115 poetry books for children, explains how poets live their lives: "At times you simply see things, concentrate on moments, get a feeling that you must capture a thought in words. Photographers take pictures, artists paint, the poet uses careful words to awaken new worlds." This book will help you and your students discover poetry everywhere, lighting your path as you turn thoughts of trees and families and laughter into carefully crafted poems. Lee's poem, "Why Poetry?," is a great one to read to your class in the days preceding the launch of this unit.

Why Poetry?
by Lee Bennett Hopkins

Why poetry?
Why?
Why sunsets?
Why trees?
Why birds?
Why seas?
Why you?
Why me?
Why friends?
Why families?
Why laugh?
Why cry?
Why hello?
Why good-bye?
Why poetry?

That's why!

The first day of any new unit begins with a generous invitation. We considered inviting children to read and reread poems, set words to music, and perform a few poems so those poems got into their bones. We weighed the idea of helping children study a single poem closely, collecting their observations about that poem and the genre. In the end, our first priority was to create a context in which poetry would grow. We wanted to invite children to give respectful, reverent attention to the details of their lives. Saul Bellow, a Nobel Laureate of literature says that to write, people must connect with their "observing instrument." He says, "There is that observing instrument in us—in childhood, at any rate—at the sight of a man's face, his shoes, the color of light . . . From this source come words, phrases, syllables."

We decided to launch this unit by teaching children to use all their senses, plus their hearts and minds and imaginations, to take in the details of their lives in fresh ways. We did this by creating a museum of objects in the classroom and inviting children to marvel at the mysteries of these objects, as suggested by the poet Patricia Hubbell. She writes, "When I was ten years old, I started a museum in the playhouse in our backyard. I filled the shelves with birds' nests, rocks, shells, pressed wildflowers . . . About the time I started the museum, I began to write poems . . . Birds' nests and rocks, leaves and butterflies found their way into the poems."

You may wonder why we scaffold children's topic choices today. This is an intentional departure from the design of the writing workshop. The rationale is that children will write more precisely and poetically about topics that matter to them once they've first learned how to see and to hear like a poet. At the end of the day, you'll invite children to bring in objects of their own choice to write about in tomorrow's share, using line breaks to convey the big feeling it gives them. Thus they will progress in steps toward Session 3, when they mine their lives for topics that matter and write to convey that meaning.

You will find that when teaching a unit on poetry, you use more figurative language and speak in more poetic ways during your minilessons than you do when teaching other units. Your language will be part of your broader effect to create a context in which poetry will grow, immersing children in fresh, precise language. You will speak metaphorically as you teach, engaging students in playful, innovative, and sometimes abstract uses of language. In today's session we speak of "poets' eyes" to suggest that poets see things in unusual ways; and this way of seeing becomes the seeds of a poem.

Today also begins the building of a collection of mentor poems. Throughout this unit we will refer to the folder of mentor texts that children will study and annotate throughout the unit. If you are able to get permissions to copy a small collection of poems so that students can have them to reference and annotate, we've found that children benefit from access to poems they can touch and mark up. Some teachers create a stapled packet of mentor poems for the unit, and others clear a space on a bulletin board or wall to post the poems that students are studying. We tend to include any mentor text we use in minilessons, and any others that resonate for students

during other times in the day. Of course, your class's poetry folders will look different from ours, because you'll include poems that you or your students bring in or fall in love with throughout the unit. The poetry folders function both as a collection of mentor texts and as sort of a poetry portrait of your class. To get you started, we'll include printable versions of a few of the mentor poems we use in the sessions in the online resources, knowing that you will undoubtedly add to your own class's collections as you see fit.

Note: The online resources include some information that is useful for this unit. You might want to print the bibliography of recommended poetry books to borrow from your library or visit some of the suggested digital resources. You will also find poetry paper, poems by Zoë Ryder White and Amy Ludwig VanDerwater, and a handful of student poems.

Seeing with Poets' Eyes

CONNECTION

Celebrate the way the class has immersed itself in poetry, and tell children that today you'll teach them to see the world in fresh ways, like poets do.

I had a basket of treasures by my feet when I invited children to come to the meeting area. I heard some of their curious whispers as they found their seats. I began, "Writers, today is an important day. We have been reading lots of poems together all year, and poems have been sprouting up all over our classroom—on our walls and windows and doors. Our room has been getting ready for *us* to be poets!

"Today I'm going to talk to you about your eyesight. How many of you wear glasses or contacts?" A few hands went up. "Well, today I am going to suggest that to write poetry, every one of you needs to wear glasses." I slid my reading glasses on to accentuate my point. "Not reading glasses, and not glasses that help if you are near- or farsighted. But poets' glasses. A poet's special lenses." Shifting away from preaching, I said, "Let me show you what I mean. Right now, will each of you replay in your mind your trip to school this morning?" I gave the children a few seconds of silence to start. "Think about what you saw." Then I said, "Tell your partner what you saw." I listened to what a few children saw on their way to school.

I called the class back together. "You all saw *a lot* of things on your way to school—buses, kids, the trees. Nora even said that she saw a cricket jump across the sidewalk in front of her! You saw these things with your regular eyes. But I have a secret to share. Poets don't see things with regular eyes. They see the world differently! In our new unit, you are going to have to put on a poet's lenses, to see with a poets' eyes. This is important because much of a poet's work comes *before* pencil touches paper."

❧ Name the teaching point.

"Today I want to teach you that poets see with poets' eyes. Poets look at things with their hearts and minds. They sometimes look at things from different angles or think about what things resemble. This helps poets write about the world in different, unusual ways."

◆ COACHING

This bend assumes that you have had a chance to immerse children in poetry prior to the unit. If you haven't actually been reading poems all year and if there aren't poems all over your classroom, you will, of course, alter this lead a bit. One alternative is to talk about the fact that poems are read at important times—at weddings, graduations, Martin Luther King's Day. Poetry is the genre we turn to when our hearts are breaking and when our hearts are especially full. In her wise book, Awakening the Heart, *Georgia Heard writes, "A classroom environment can send out messages: that all of our students' lives matter; that every voice is worth listening to; and that students can take risks in writing poems about whatever their hearts urge them to write. I focus on creating the emotional environment first, and then I trust that the poems will follow."*

Although you'll stress to children that they put on their special "poet's lenses," the reality is that children are natural observers all on their own. Picasso once said, "It took me four years to paint like Raphael, but a lifetime to paint like a child." Imagine the three-year-old child who describes the snowflakes stuck to his woolen mitten. "Look!" he exclaims. "Snow bugs!"

TEACHING

Show the children how one poet saw an object in a different, unusual way, contrasting it with the "regular" way someone might see the same object.

"For starters, use your regular eyes to take a quick look at our pencil sharpener." A few children cocked their heads, puzzled at such an odd request. "You'll see why in a minute. Take a look at it, and get ready to share what you see." I looked intently at it myself. After a few seconds I asked children to turn and talk about what they saw.

"It's gray and square," said Silas. "I see different-sized holes in the front," added Rowan. I called them back together and shared my own observations. "What I see is a gray box, a machine that makes my pencil sharp." I used flat intonation to suggest this was a bland way to see.

"We've just looked at the pencil sharpener with regular eyes. Now, let's look at how Zoë saw it with her poets' eyes." I turned over a page on my chart pad to reveal the poem. "As you read, pay special attention to how Zoë sees the world in a fresh, new way." I gave them a moment to read the poem, and then I read it aloud. Some of them joined in.

Pencil Sharpener
by Zoë Ryder White

I think there are a hundred bees
inside the pencil sharpener
and they buzz
and buzz
and buzz
until my point
is sharp!

Highlight the novelty in the poet's vision, thinking aloud about how she might have done this.

"Poets, when I read this poem, I was so surprised! I didn't think about our pencil sharpener at all like Zoë describes it! I just saw a machine that makes my pencil sharp. But Zoë sees the pencil sharpener like a poet sees it, in a fresh, new way! She imagines that there are *bees* inside the pencil sharpener and that they are buzzing around the tip of her pencil to make it sharp! Imagine that! This poem makes *me* see our classroom pencil sharpener in a fresh, new way, and that's what poetry can do. It opens our eyes to new ways of seeing. It's interesting to think, '*How* did she do this?' I think she thought about what the pencil sharpener looks like, what it does—even what it sounds like—and then she might've thought, 'That reminds me of bees!'"

The truth is that you can, of course, see more poetry in a pencil sharpener than you let on, but if you say, "That just looks like a gray box to me," you name what many of your children see. This way you can demonstrate what it means to alter your vision and learn to see more.

While this book contains a handful of poems for you to use, it's even better if you can enrich your classroom poetry library, because the best poetry teachers are the poems themselves. Many of you will have purchased Kristine O'Connell George's book Old Elm Speaks: Tree Poems *as part of the trade pack to go with this book. Kristine is an award-winning poet, and this collection offers many possible mentor poems for your students. We include four of her poems from* Old Elm Speaks *in this book, and we highly recommend it for your classroom library. You can see the bibliography in the online resources for other recommended poetry resources.*

One of the ways to pop out, or highlight, the point you are making is to contrast what you are saying with the alternative. That's what you do here when you highlight Zoë's imaginative vision with the alternative.

Show the class how you can practice seeing with poets' eyes by looking at a familiar object in a new way.

I pulled some scissors out of my basket of treasures and held them up. "With my regular eyes I see a pair of scissors." Ramon nodded in agreement "You do, too, Ramon?" Now the rest of the kids were nodding. "Oh, you, too? All of you? Wow. So our regular eyes seem to see the same thing. Let's all try now to switch our way of seeing and to see these scissors with poets' eyes. Think about what you see, what these scissors may remind you of. If you get any ideas, put your thumbs on your knees." I began to turn and manipulate the scissors, and as I did, I mulled over possible ways to see them, as if weighing options. "I see a fish with a big eye. I see a butterfly. I see a hungry shark! It's sneaking up on its prey and then—*snap*!" I snapped the scissors closed on an imaginary fish.

"Did you see how by comparing the scissors to other things, we looked at the scissors in completely new and fresh ways? It helped when we made the scissors move too, didn't it, and thought about what they do. Did you see with poets' eyes?" Enthusiastic thumbs started popping up. I knew the children were ready to try this on their own.

ACTIVE ENGAGEMENT

Ask the children to think of how they would write with poets' eyes about another object. Then show what the poet did.

"Zoë wrote another poem, this one about the ceiling. Would you look at our ceiling right now? Try looking with poets' eyes, seeing it in a fresh, new way." I looked intently at the ceiling.

"Tell your partner what you see when you look at the ceiling with poets' eyes."

Immediately the room filled with talk. A couple of children looked around, seeming a bit unsure, so I piped in with a little coaching. "Think about what the ceiling looks like, or reminds you of. Think about what we use it for. Think of different things it could be." I listened in to a few partnerships, noting children's comfort level with the concept of poets' eyes.

"It's like . . . like . . . a flat wall," said Rob

"The ceiling makes me feel safe!" said Owen.

"It's protecting us from rain," said Rowan.

"It's our lid," said Silas.

If the teaching component of the minilesson had ended before this section, you would have said to children, "Do this." You would not have told them how to do it. This is the procedural part of the minilesson.

Poet Kristine O'Connell George saw trees with poets' eyes when writing Old Elm Speaks. *She says, "I'm a tree lover and a tree hugger, which inspired me to write poems about trees. In writing* Old Elm Speaks, *I spent so much time with trees (sitting in trees, sitting under trees, visiting trees at parks and arboretums) that I came to see trees as beings that might talk to me and tell me something of their lives. I saw the important role trees played in the landscape of our lives and memories."*

Ask children to turn and talk with their partners before you elicit responses from particular individuals. Again, we do this to allow every child to be active and interactive. If you simply call on the children who raise their hands, only a handful of children will do the mental work of producing their own responses to your questions.

"Wow! Your poets' eyes are in perfect working order! Okay, let's read Zoë's poem and pay special attention to the fresh, new way *she* saw the ceiling." I read "Ceiling" to the class as the children followed along.

Ceiling

by Zoë Ryder White

The ceiling
is the sky
for the classroom.

Debrief, highlighting the transferable point you are making. Poets see in fresh ways by looking closely, by caring about what they see, and sometimes by making comparisons.

"Poets, did you notice how Zoë saw the ceiling differently than most of us? This is what is so important about our poets' eyes—we don't often see the same thing! Like Zoë, you didn't just say what you saw with regular eyes. No way! You really thought about what the ceiling looks like, what it reminds you of!

"Poets see the world in ways the rest of us would never have imagined. They look at the world closely and carefully; they look with their hearts and their minds. They try to let an ordinary ceiling matter to them."

LINK

Send your students off to study objects you've brought (feathers, shells, and so on) and to see them in fresh, new ways.

I picked up the basket of objects and put it on my lap. "I know you've been curious about my basket of things. I have a basket like this for each table. Each one contains lots of objects that you can look at with poets' eyes. These are objects you've seen before with your regular eyes. And today you'll have a chance to practice using your poets' eyes to see them differently. Some objects are things you've seen before in this room, like the scissors, and others are things I have found here and there over the last couple of weeks, like this interesting pebble. Whatever you select, try to see that object in fresh, new ways!

"At each of your tables, you will also find brand-new poetry folders, special clipboards, and paper for recording what you see when you look at an object or two with poets' eyes. You won't start writing *poems* just yet. For now, find an interesting thing to look at and write what you see. Off you go!"

As children began working, I voiced over, calling, "Challenge yourself to look at the object for a long time and to think about it in unusual ways. Remember, turn it around, move it, listen to the sounds."

We selected this very simple, brief poem, as we selected "Pencil Sharpener," because these are models to which children can aspire and because the dominant feature of both poems is the one we're trying to highlight. In longer, lusher poems, the poet will have done so many things that the poems won't illustrate our point as well as this one does—that poets see the world with fresh, new eyes. This poem is a very sparse one, written for the purpose of this minilesson.

Today you will not yet ask children to write poems because your goal now is to focus their attention on vision and fresh language, without yet exploring line breaks and forms of poetry. That would be too much for one minilesson. Some of your children, though, might experiment with turning their observations into the beginnings of poems. You can support these students during your conferences and small-group work.

Usually you don't send children off with instructions to spend the entire writing workshop doing what you assign. Instead, minilessons usually end with you reminding children to add what you've taught to their repertoire and, meanwhile, to continue their ongoing work. Today's send-off is different from usual. You are setting children up to observe with poets' eyes and jot down observations.

After another few minutes, I voiced over again, saying, "Think about what your object reminds you of. That is one way to help grow your poets' eyes." I added, "You'll probably have time today to do this work with two or three objects from your basket.

"I'm going to set the timer for ten minutes. We often look at things quickly, but think how much more you'll see by spending more time with one object. Then you'll have time to do this with one or two more objects.

"After this, for the rest of your life, whenever you want to write a poem, remember that you need to see the world with poets' eyes. Stretch your imagination and look in ways that are brand new. You don't want to just write, 'The pine cone is brown.' It *is* brown, but we can all see that with our regular eyes. Someone using poets' eyes might write, 'The pine cone is a wooden porcupine' or 'The pine cone is a tree for an elf.'

"When the timer goes off, you can share with your writing partner for a minute. Green table, get started."

Getting writers to study a single object for a long stretch of time is challenging. In courses for professional writers, people are sometimes asked to spend a full day describing an egg in its shell or an eggplant. To write well, it is important to learn to look long and close and to notice what others would pass by.

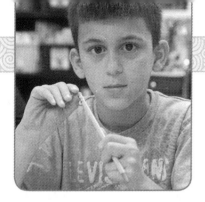
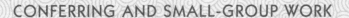

Seeing through Your Own Unique Poets' Eyes

BY NOW, YOU KNOW THAT AT THE START OF ANY NEW UNIT, it is especially important for you to move rapidly among writers, rallying as many as possible to be enthralled with the new work. The challenge you've issued today is not especially demanding, so you will probably find that the most important thing you can do is to help children work zealously toward high standards. If a child seems to be scrawling down the first phrases that come to mind after observing an acorn, you might ask if his strategy is to brainstorm everything that comes to mind and only afterward reread the list to select the items that seem exactly right. If a child seems to be seeing only the most obvious traits in an object, join the youngster in studying the object, and model how to give rapt attention to it. Carry with you some sketches and jottings made by children from previous years, and invite a table of youngsters to talk about how one does this work *really* well.

It's important for children to feel successful right from the beginning of a new unit of study. You will want to approach today's writing time knowing that today's work may feel abstract or unnatural for some writers and that these children will benefit from learning some other possible ways to see with writer's eyes. When Rob, for example, looked at the shell, he saw a shell. Not a tiny mouse ear or a boat for a ladybug—*a shell.*

I sat next to Rob and watched as he sketched his shell from different perspectives, jotting the words *smooth, sharp,* and *curly* among his drawings. Rob is articulate and observant, but he resists translating his thoughts into writing because he is afraid "it won't be good." Many of my conferences encourage him to take a risk. I opened the conference by asking him a question that by now the students had come to expect. "Hi, Rob. How's your writing going today?"

"Fine." That was all he offered. I knew there was more, so I pressed on.

"Rob, you know lots about writing. Remember, when I ask how it's going, I know you can give details about what you're *working on* as a writer. Let's start over. Hi, Rob. How's it going with your writing today?"

"Fine. I mean, I'm observing this shell and writing down what I notice." He kept working on his tiny shell sketches.

"Ah, I see." I put my hand over Rob's to stop his sketching, to get his attention. Then I said, "I can tell that you've thought about exactly what you see and feel with this shell. I also notice the way you've looked at this shell from one angle, here," I pointed, "and from another angle, here." I added, "That is exactly what I was talking about in the lesson, when I said that it helps to look at something from different angles."

MID-WORKSHOP TEACHING Slowing Down and Lingering with an Object to See—and Write—More

After just five minutes or so, I stood in the midst of the writers and interrupted. "Poets, can I stop you for a minute? I was just talking with Nina, and we discovered something important. She was observing the stapler, and she wrote, 'It's like a shark. It's like a diving board. It's like an alligator.' She was definitely seeing the stapler with poets' eyes, right? But something was missing. Then she said, 'I'm just going to stick with one of these and see what happens.' So she asked herself *how* the stapler is like an alligator and wrote, 'The stapler snaps open and closed. It has little silver teeth. It bites my words and keeps my ideas together.' Can you hear the difference?

"Many of you are looking at your object in one way, then in another way, then another way, just like Nina was. You are saying, 'The leaf is like a little fan.' Then you go to a totally *different* way and say, 'The leaf is like grass.' Then you try yet *another* way of looking and say, 'The leaf is like a little tree.'

"What I want to tell you is *slow down.* If you say the leaf is like a little tree, look again at the leaf. *How* is it like a little tree? Do the veins look like branches? How can you describe the color of green in that leaf? Give it a try."

"But I'm done doing that now. I don't know what to do," he sighed. Rob had little more than a labeled sketch to show for his work.

"Oh, dear! So, Rob, I have a question. Why, when I asked how your writing is going, did you say 'Fine'? If you don't know what to do, that can't feel *fine*. I bet it's kind of frustrating for you."

"Yeah. Well, I'm not sure if I really can see this shell in a new way. I was trying, but I didn't see anything. It's a shell. I see a shell."

"Did you say 'Fine' because you thought I might be disappointed that you didn't see a mouse's ear or something?"

He nodded, looking slightly crestfallen.

"Rob, I get frustrated all the time in my writing, too. And I find myself not knowing what to do or how to get my ideas onto the paper. Lots of writers feel that way! Plus, you actually did something important. I think that realizing a strategy isn't working for you—and realizing that's a problem—is a big deal. This allows you to think, 'Are there *other* strategies I could try?' Because there are lots of possible ways to achieve your real goal, which is to look at the world as a poet does, seeing with fresh eyes."

I decided that offering Rob a new strategy would not only give him an opportunity to get unstuck, but would also get more strategies going in the room so that other students could benefit from Rob's work. I said, "Let me suggest another strategy poets sometimes use and see if it works for you. Poets sometimes think not 'Can I compare this with something—a mouse's ear or what not?' but instead, they think, 'Does this remind me of something, of a memory?'"

After studying, he said, "Hey, yeah! It reminds me of a shell I found one time. There were a whole bunch of shells that all looked kind of the same, but I just picked one of them. It was shiny inside, like this one."

"Wow, I can almost see it, how it was shiny on the inside. Being observant like that is important. To me it sounds like you could have the beginning of a poem, don't you think? Rob, I know you want to do *exactly* what I talked about in the lesson today, but you are spending so much time worrying, 'Am I doing the right thing?' that you aren't doing anything. Sometimes the right thing for a writer is *not* exactly what's in a minilesson."

"So, I just write down my memory of my shell?"

"Exactly! Sometimes you have to just take what's on your mind and write *that*. Tell about how you saw thousands of shells, but you didn't pick them all up. You picked up *this* one. And tell about what you saw when you looked closely at it. This will be a beautiful poem. I can feel it in my bones. I'll come back and check on you in a little while. Okay?"

After I conferred with a couple of other children, I returned to find Rob rereading the poem he had started (see Figure 1–1).

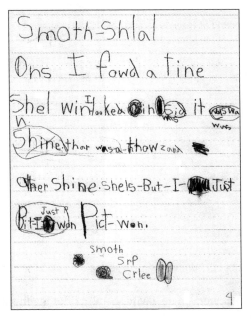

FIG. 1–1 Rob uses the memory strategy to get unstuck.

Smooth Shell

Once I found a tiny
shell. When I looked inside
it was shiny.
There was a thousand
other shiny shells but I just
picked one.
Smooth
Sharp
Curly

If a few children need some extra support early on in the unit so that they become invested in writing poetry, don't hesitate to give them a brief piggyback ride so that, with the help of very strong scaffolding, lo and behold, they will find that they are doing exemplary work. Specifically, this might mean that while most of your children are still writing their observations, you get a few started writing not only observations but also poems, and then you help those children lay their poems out in several different ways, revising them so they sound right. Children may not have gotten to this place independently, but you can nevertheless help them build a new image of themselves around the fact that they are doing magnificent work.

Celebrating First Efforts with a Symphony Share

Celebrate how children are looking at objects with poets' eyes through a symphony share.

I asked children to join me in the meeting area, clipboards in hand. Then I said, "What an exciting day! Listening to you and reading over your shoulders just now, I am seeing familiar objects in new ways.

"Quickly look over your observations and choose a favorite line—one that feels especially descriptive. When I point to you, read just that line. It's okay if it's a fragment. We're going to do this quickly, so that together, our lines form an abstract poem!"

I pointed to child after child, and soon the room filled with their words.

"The shell is a tiny pink ear."

"Lost, a sideways bowl."

"Old wood, old wood, a sailboat for a mouse!"

When the last child had shared, I whispered, "Writers, you are seeing the world like poets do!"

Tell children that they have important work to do. Invite them to offer feedback on their partner's writing.

"Now that we've celebrated ourselves, we have work to do. Poems are beautiful—so it's easy to hear one and say, simply, 'How lovely.' But you all know by now that every piece of writing, whether it's a narrative or a lab report or a review, can always be improved. If each one of you is to become the best poet you can be, it's essential that you give and receive valuable feedback.

"So right now, trade clipboards with your partner and read his or her work, with poets' eyes, ready to offer both specific compliments and specific suggestions for how the writing you've read can become even better. Here are a few things you might consider as you read." I revealed a chart I'd started, titled "Reading Poetry Like a Poet."

Sharing just one line this way teaches children to pinpoint places where their writing is especially strong, places where they are learning to see and write with poets' eyes. It also keeps their writing alive for more revision because sometimes writers feel already published, less interested in revision after sharing a whole piece with the group.

> ### Reading Poetry Like a Poet
> - As I read this writing, can I make a picture in my mind?
> - Does this writing help me look at something in the world in new ways?
> - Does this writing give me a certain feeling or make me think or question?

I gave children a minute to read one another's work, before calling out, "Now turn and talk to your partner. First, say one *specific* thing about the writing that works well. Not, 'This is nice' or 'I like it' but 'The line . . . makes me think/feel/ wonder . . . ' or 'The way so and so phrased this reminds me . . . '"

After a minute, I said, "If you haven't done so already, try to offer your partner a bit of specific advice for how to make his or her writing even better. Could the images be clearer? More unusual? Might your partner add something so that the writing makes you think or feel or wonder something? Be your best poetry critics!"

Close the session by inviting children to think about other objects they would like to observe closely, either from the classroom, outside, or even from home. Invite children to bring these special treasures to class to add to their treasure baskets.

"Wow, I heard such great suggestions and such great ways to make your writing even better. Today, as you go off to recess, think about other objects you would like to add to your treasure baskets. Look out for special objects that *you* want to study closely, objects you want to look at with your poets' eyes. These might be things you have at home, or they might be things you find outside, just like the pebble I found. Bring these objects in tomorrow, and we'll add them to your baskets! And get ready to start paying attention, seeing like poets. A poet named Joyce Sidman said, "Here's the secret of poetry: the poems are already inside you. They are waiting. All the things you think, and feel, and notice (that's what poems are, after all) are waiting for the right words to set them free."

Listening for Line Breaks

IN THIS SESSION, you'll teach students that poets are intentional about their line breaks, trying out a few different ways until their words look and sound right to them.

GETTING READY

✓ "Aquarium" by Valerie Worth, enlarged on chart paper, copied once with line breaks and once without (see Teaching)

✓ "Reading Poetry Like a Poet" chart from Session 1, to add to during the active engagement

✓ Mentor poems in poetry folders (or on poetry wall or poetry bulletin board) (see Link)

✓ "Between Two Trees" by Kristine O'Connell George, enlarged on chart paper (see Share)

Task:
Choose favorite line.
- feels really
    descriptive
- point & read out loud

Task
If you wand to get
better as a poet, you
must get feedback.
- get with table partners
- go over anchor

TODAY YOU INTRODUCE ANOTHER ELEMENT OF POETRY—sound. You'll announce that poems are written to be read aloud, and you'll show children how poets play with line breaks to influence the way poems sound.

One way to highlight the decisions poets make is to set children up to engage in a close reading of a published poem, examining how it was made. Your children have lots of experience studying mentor texts, noticing what the author has done and thinking, "Can I try similar work in my writing?" Today you will remind them that they can read poems just this way, asking, "How is this poem made? What has this poet done?" This work is essential to the work your second-graders must do to meet world-class standards for reading.

While this lesson focuses on using line breaks to affect a poem's sound, an implicit additional goal is to teach children to use line breaks in ways that convey meaning. You'll show that poets work hard to make their poems sound the way they want them to, and they also ask, "Does this decision fit with my intended meaning?" This session is ambitious. Your children won't entirely grasp these concepts, but a minilesson, like a piece of literature, can inspire and uplift even if it's not concrete in a child's mind. In Bend II, you'll unpack this instruction further, so children will have plenty of opportunities to grow into it.

By the end of this minilesson, you will have laid out two of the primary elements poets work with when they compose poetry: language and sound. By allowing children to focus their efforts on essential elements of crafting a poem, you lay the groundwork for children to do more sophisticated thinking and writing starting on day 3. Today children should be ready to revisit their notes on a few of the items they've observed, both yesterday and today, drafting these into poems if they didn't do so from the start and otherwise experimenting with the format of these early draft poems. The goal is that they'll explore writing their content one way and then another, moving around the line breaks and asking, "Does this way of placing my words on the page match what I'm trying to say? Does it sound the way I want it to?"

Listening for Line Breaks

CONNECTION

Share with the class some examples of fresh, new ways they've seen the world, and let them in on another element of poetry: sound.

"Writers, I love seeing that so many of you have brought precious treasures in for your table's basket—and some of you have your own treasure boxes. You can absolutely spend time today sketching and jotting words to capture the way you see these new items with poets' eyes. Just a few minutes ago, Hana told me that leaves are like a birthday cake to a slug! Did any of you ever think of a leaf that way? I know I didn't.

"Yesterday you learned that when making a poem, poets describe what they see with their poets' eyes. Another thing poets do when they want to make a poem is to use the sounds of words to make music!

"Here's the thing, though. Poets don't sing or play instruments to make music. The music of poems comes from the sound of words and from the way the words are laid on the page. Poets choose how to place words to give the reader instructions—to tell us how poems should sound when we read them!"

❧ **Name the teaching point.**

"Today I want to teach you that one way to give your poems music is to pay attention to where you put words and where you *don't* put words. Poets try a few different ways of breaking up their lines, reading the poem aloud after each try, until the poem is written in a way that sounds just right."

TEACHING

Show a familiar poem, written as prose and as a poem, and channel children to listen as you read the prose version in a blah way.

"Let me show you what I mean." I flipped open the chart pad to reveal a poem with which the class was familiar. "Let's take a closer look at this poem, written in two ways—as prose and as the author intended. Let's read 'Aquarium' by Valerie Worth. You'll see that I've written it two different ways on chart paper. One way will sound like I'm telling you

You may be thinking, "My children would never say something like Hana said." But you can make these jewels happen. If one of your children looked at the snail and said, "That guy loves to eat!" you could respond, "The leaves are probably like a . . . a . . . dessert to the slug." The child will probably add something like, "Yeah, the leaves are like ice cream. The leaves are like a birthday cake." Later, you repeat what the child said without mentioning that you coauthored the metaphor.

When we've taught this, some children have looked at us in what can only be described as utter confusion. We expect this. Line breaks are an abstract concept. We knew that children would come to a much better understanding if we showed them a strong example and gave them a chance to play around with a poem.

Of course, you don't need to use this particular poem. Use another if you prefer.

something. The other way will sound like music. Listen, and you'll see what I mean. First, I'm going to read the prose version."

Goldfish flash gold and silver scales;
they flick and slip away under green weed—
But round brown snails stick to the glass and stay.

Goldfish
Flash
Gold and silver scales;
They flick and slip away
Under green weed—
But round brown snails
Stick
To the glass
And stay.

Read the prose version as if you're simply reporting on what these sea creatures do; read it in a monotone voice, not with expression.

Read the actual poem with special attention to the placement of words, so that children can hear the rhythm, emphases, and pauses—so that they can hear the "music" in this poem.

"This layout," I pointed to the prose version, "tells us to read this just like we're talking to each other. Because all the words go across the page, we read this like we're telling someone that we went to the store and bought some gum or something. It's kind of like blah, blah, blah. Partner 1, read this version to Partner 2." They did.

Contrast this with reading the same poem written with the line breaks the author intended. Discuss why the line breaks support the meaning and influence your reading.

"Now, on the other hand, look at this version!" I gestured to where I'd written the poem as Valerie Worth intended, with line breaks. "This is how we're accustomed to seeing this poem, right? Let me read it with line breaks, and will you notice how different it sounds?" I read aloud the poem, with great expression so that children could hear its "music" the way Valerie Worth intended. I emphasized stand-alone words, such as "Flash" and "Stick," paused after them to account for the white space, and conveyed the rhythm in phrases such as "They flick and slip away."

"When we read the poem *with* line breaks, it sounds different, doesn't it? When Valerie Worth divided the words into lines, she gave us unspoken instructions for how to read them. Partner 2, try reading the correct version of the poem to your partner. You'll see, I think, that the line breaks make you read it so your voice moves like a fish swims." I moved my hand down the print, snaking my hand around like a fish would swerve through the water. "All these words are in a fish-like line down the page, with the lines going back and forth, flicking this way and that."

After children read the poem to each other, I said, "You can think about why Valerie made the decisions she did. Like notice that in this line, she put 'flick' and 'slip away' on one line, 'They flick and slip away' to show that in one instant, the fish are there *and* gone. By the next line, all we see is green weed."

Then I said, "She can also show how some things slow . . . down . . . like . . . a . . . snail." I pointed to that part of the poem. Down here the snails aren't moving. They stick . . . to the glass . . . and stay. Do you see how the line breaks tell me how to use my voice when I'm reading the poem? That's one of the ways Valerie Worth gave this poem music."

When you and your children study a text in a minilesson, it is almost always a familiar text. We have written the new, prose-like version of Valerie's poem on chart paper for the purpose of today's minilesson, displaying it alongside the actual poem. The brevity of this poem is intentional. In every minilesson, you will always want to think about ways to make your point in less time.

When I have something to say to children, I don't hesitate to do so. If I tried to extract these same observations from the class, it would have taken me exponentially longer to make my point, and the lesson could easily have been buried in a lot of convoluted questioning. On the other hand, I do need to worry whether children are really listening to and "getting" what I try to teach. I use the visual support of the written poem and my gestures, an expressive voice, and eye contact, and I give them chances to read aloud. I share the fun to make it likely that they are mentally with me!

ACTIVE ENGAGEMENT

Ask the children to read the poem aloud again, using line breaks as the author instructed them to do. Challenge them to reflect on how the line breaks influenced their oral reading.

"Try reading the first part—the fast, flitty-fish part—of the poem again to your partner, reading quickly, and then read this slow snail part." As I pointed to the top and the bottom halves of the poem, I let my voice change from a flighty fish to a slow snail. "When you read aloud, notice how Valerie Worth makes you read the snail part differently."

The way you give instructions provides the children with a lot of guidance!

The room erupted with voices reading and then discussing. After two minutes I signaled them back together. "I heard you read it in so many ways! Everyone was paying attention to Valerie's line breaks. What I want to know is how were the line breaks telling your voice what to do? Think about that, and show me a thumb when you're ready to talk about it." I gave them a minute or so to consider my question, then asked them to turn and talk. This time the discussion was a little calmer, as it often is when the work is more complex. I listened in on a couple of partnerships.

"Well, the first two lines seem like a special announcement or something, so I say, 'Goldfish! Flash!' like 'Hey! Look at this!'" Silas explained.

"It makes me say, 'Flick and slip away' fast, but when I see, 'Stick,' all by itself I want to slow down," Rob replied.

Summarize what you want the children to learn.

"What I want you to notice is that Valerie Worth—like most poets—uses line breaks to help her readers find the music in her poem. She uses line breaks to help us read her words like quick fish and like slow snails. So, we have studied another question to ask as we read poems," I said as I added this to our anchor chart.

Reading Poetry Like a Poet

- As I read this writing, can I make a picture in my mind?
- Does this writing help me look at something in the world in new ways?
- Does this writing give me a certain feeling or make me think or question?
- Does this poem have music?

LINK

Remind the children that they have options, including the option to observe with poets' eyes, to turn notes into poems, or to rewrite poems with line breaks.

"Today, poets, as you go back to your centers and to your precious objects—including the ones you brought in from home, you can continue seeing with poets' eyes and collecting notes for new poems, and you can also take some of the notes you wrote yesterday and start turning them into poems with line breaks. You'll probably write each poem a few different ways before you find the music you like best. After this, any day when you write poems, remember that you're trying to turn words into music—and line breaks can help you do that. You can also study the mentor poems in your folders, if you like, to see how other poets are making decisions about line breaks and how those decisions change the music of their poems."

If your children are studying mentor texts on a poetry wall or poetry bulletin board instead of in folders, of course you'll direct their attention there, instead.

In your minilessons, you will want try to leave children aware of their options. You will try to expand children's repertoire of strategies rather than assign a particular strategy to all children.

Hearing More in the Music of Poetry
A Strategy Lesson with Advanced Students

INEVITABLY, YOUR ROOM WILL BE FILLED WITH A RANGE OF WRITERS, from those who struggle to comprehend the form of a poem (hopefully not many!) to those who suddenly see poems everywhere. While your tendency may be to prioritize the strugglers, don't meanwhile neglect your more advanced writers. You may want to pull this latter group together for a strategy lesson, helping them channel the many things they are noticing about the craft and sound of poetry into their writing.

You could revisit Valerie Worth's poem "Aquarium," which you used during today's teaching, and ask them what else they notice her doing. They may, for example, realize that she uses not just line breaks to give readers hints to how her poem should sound, but rhyme: *away* and *stay*. While this is the only rhyme in the poem, the kids may realize that it, too, adds to the sound, or rhythm, of the poem. Especially observant children will realize that although they don't rhyme, the word pairs *flick* and *slip*, *green* and *weed*, and *round* and *brown* sound alike and thus add to the sound of the poem too. While you won't encourage these kids to now all try their hand at rhyming (expect poems that favor sound over meaning, if you do), you will want to acknowledge that rhyming is one fun tool poets use—and it can help to add emphasis to certain words.

Children may also notice that punctuation in poems also tips the reader off to say or hear the poem a certain way. In "Aquarium," a semicolon and a hyphen achieve two distinct purposes. The semicolon joins the line before it with the one after it. Chances are, your second-graders haven't yet learned the purpose or use of this form of punctuation, but there is no harm in quickly establishing that this particular form of punctuation connects the two lines it comes between. Then you could move on to say that periods, commas, and question marks—all forms of punctuation second-graders know—can be used to indicate how to read a poem, and ask them to think about how those other forms of punctuation might change the sound of this poem. The hyphen tells the reader to pause, and there's a clear divide between the sound of the first part of the poem, and the sound of the second part, as the class already discussed during the minilesson. You might ask this group to imagine other reasons a poet might want their readers to pause.

The hyphen is a terrific segue into a discussion of the opposite of sound: silence. You might want to share another poem with this group that makes use of white space to indicate a pause, a breath, or silence. Have them think about how silence, too, is a kind of sound and think about when and why a writer would want to introduce silence into a poem.

This is sophisticated work, so don't be surprised if not all of your second-graders are up for it immediately. They will be eventually, and for the time being, it's important to engage those who are. There is so much to notice in even the simplest poem, and you'll want all kids in your class to see as much as they can.

MID-WORKSHOP TEACHING
Writing a Poem Several Different Ways

Standing among the writers, I said, "Poets, can I stop all of you? I want to tell you about the brilliant work Zach is doing. Zach is turning his notes about a leaf into a poem. First he reread his notes and crossed out 'the boring parts' (that's the way he put it), and then he looked at the leaf again with poets' eyes, finding more to say about his leaf. Then he took his words and ideas and wrote them one way on the page—see, look." I held up one version. "Then he reread them *again*, and do you know what he said? He said, 'Wait a minute. Hmm,' *and he wrote them another way*! So far he has used line breaks to write about the leaf in three different ways! That is exactly what poets do.

"Would you all get with your partner and talk over how you could write one of *your* poems? Remember to think not only about *how* it might go but also about *why* it might go that way. Okay?"

Using Line Breaks to Highlight Meaning

Introduce the idea that line breaks not only create music, but can also highlight special parts or words in poems.

"Writers, will you please bring your poems from today over to the rug with you?"

After the students had convened in the meeting area, I said, "Writers, today we studied and worked with something very important in poems—line breaks. When you write stories, you think about where to begin new paragraphs. But when you write poems, you think about where to begin every single line. Sometimes a poet will choose to place one word all by itself. This is a hint to readers that the word is very important. By placing white space around a word—leaving the word all by itself—a poet helps a reader know that this line really matters."

Set children up to reflect on the line breaks in "Between Two Trees" by Kristine O'Connell George, particularly the lines with only one word.

Let's look at Kristine O'Connell George's poem, 'Between Two Trees.' See how the words *Summer, between,* and *hammock* each stand on a line all by themselves? By doing this, Kristine is telling her readers to slow down and pay close attention to these words. Listen as I read this poem." I read the poem aloud, focusing on the meaning brought out through the line breaks.

Between Two Trees
Kristine O'Connell George

Summer
fills the
empty space
between
two trees
with a
hammock.

We begin this unit with teaching children about line breaks because this visual aspect of poetry is one that can help children quickly feel that they have written poems. Students who are used to writing sentences all across the page may forget to make line breaks as they write. This share, focusing on how a poet can think about line breaks after writing—during revision—will give children a chance to think about how shape affects meaning.

When you read a poem aloud, read it for meaning, pausing lightly at the ends of lines. Be careful not to read the poem in a sing-song voice, halting for a long time at the end of each line. We want our students to understand that meaning is primary in a poem. Our thoughtful oral reading of poetry will determine the way that children read poems aloud.

"Did you hear how the line breaks influenced how I read the poem? Kristine chose to use line breaks so that the words *Summer*, *between*, and *hammock* stood alone, and because of that, those words felt more important, or more special, didn't they? They stood alone, not crowded by other words.

"When you write poems, the line breaks are like little directions to your readers. By placing a word alone, you say, 'Readers! This part is very important. Pay attention. Slow down a bit!'"

Ask students to reread their own poems from today, considering if there might be one important word that deserves its very own line. Then, invite students to share these possible new line breaks with their partners.

I paused and said, "Now, quietly reread the poems that you wrote today, asking yourself, 'Is there a very important word, a word that matters so much that I want to place it on a line all by itself?' You might find a part of your poem that you want to be read slowly or a part that just feels very special or a part that repeats or makes a certain rhythm. Those words might want lines of their very own."

I gave children a minute to reread their poems and then said, "Poets, turn and share with your partner if you have a word in your poem that deserves its own line. Tell your partner why you think you might change the line breaks to give that word more space."

The room filled with talk of possible stand-alone words, and after sharing a few of their examples, I reminded them that these decisions are important to all poets.

"Writers, tomorrow we will all write more poems, and I will be interested to see how you use line breaks to show your readers where to slow down, how you highlight some words by giving them their very own lines."

Throughout this unit, as children continue to revise for line breaks, you can help them do so by showing them to how to make slashes after words to indicate the ends of lines. If a young poet wishes to add a line break, she can simply place a slash after the word that will end the line. It is not necessary to rewrite a whole poem every time the poet wants to add a line break. That can all come at the end, at publication time.

Putting Powerful Thoughts in Tiny Packages

IN THIS SESSION, you'll teach students that poets choose topics that mean a lot to them, and then they anchor those topics in a meaningful small moment, image, or object.

GETTING READY

✔ Your own big idea and small moment to demonstrate generating ideas for poems (see Teaching)

✔ "Strategies Poets Use to Write Poems" chart (see Teaching)

✔ A big idea or big feeling that your class shares to practice generating ideas for poems. We use loving to listen to a book (see Active Engagement)

✔ Chart paper and marker (see Active Engagement)

✔ Excerpt from "Valentine for Ernest Mann" by Naomi Nye, enlarged on chart paper (see Share)

✔ Tiny Topics notepads, either recycled from earlier in the year or brand-new (see Share)

THIS LESSON SHINES A SPOTLIGHT on an essential element of poetry—meaning. Today you teach children how to choose topics for poems in such a way that they pay attention to both craft and meaning, and above all, to the intersection of the two. Up until now, your children have been writing poems about a handful of small objects—little treasures—set up around the classroom. Topic choice hasn't been a big concern, even when kids added objects of their own choice. Instead, the focus has been on writing with the sound and shape of poetry.

But we know, of course, that poets write from the heart about topics they hold dear. Today, then, you'll take your writers squarely back to the importance of writing about subjects that matter. You'll do this in ways that maintain the importance of writing with precision. Your goal will be to help children write about big topics that matter while still writing with tiny details.

In this session you'll demonstrate a way to generate a topic by thinking first of a big feeling or idea and then of a small moment, object, or image that holds that feeling, that idea. Prepare some ideas ahead of time instead of trying to come up with them on the fly. You may find that it will take some thought; you may need to kiss a few frogs before you find the prince. The key is that your feeling is big, your detail small and specific, and both are relevant to your students. You might even reverse the order of big and small, showing that a writer can notice that an object, moment, or image resurfaces often in his or her mind and can then explore its larger significance.

The suggestion that poets write about something big that is also small is hugely significant and pertains to most (or all) writing, not just to poetry. If a writer starts with something small, it's helpful for that writer to reach for something big in which to couch it (the image of a blue plastic dinosaur in the mud holds my feeling of frustration at having to share my room with a careless sibling). On the other hand, if a writer starts with something big (loving my mom), it's wise for the writer to reach next for something small (a surprise fruit gummy in my lunchbox).

Putting Powerful Thoughts in Tiny Packages

CONNECTION

Recall and celebrate what your children have been doing as poets. Tell them poets also choose their own topics.

"Writers, we have learned about two important elements of poetry. You've used your poets' eyes to see the world in fresh ways, and you've learned that line breaks are one way to give poems music. Today I want to teach you about something else that poets consider when they want to write a poem—and this is even *before* they think about how to describe something or how to position the words on the page. And this is a biggie. Poets choose topics that matter to them." I paused to be sure all eyes were on me.

"You've been writing about little treasures and other interesting objects. Poets *do* often write about shells and pine cones and even safety pins! But in real life, poets aren't told, 'Here's a pine cone. Go write a poem about it.' Instead, a poet—like every other kind of writer—needs to start by thinking, 'What matters to *me*?'"

❖ **Name the teaching point.**

"Today I'm going to teach you that poets think about a big idea, a big feeling, and then find the small moment, image, or object that holds that big feeling, that big idea."

TEACHING

Point out that poets need to find a topic that is big and that is also small and specific. Show how you generate such a topic.

"To get a good poem, I need a topic that is big—at least it needs to feel big to me, a topic that fills my heart. When I have my big, strong idea or feeling, I then think about a small moment or even just a picture in my mind—a sound or an object—that gives me that feeling. Right now I want to show you how I can start with something big, like how much I adore my niece Katie. That's a big topic that gives me a big feeling."

Writing a poem requires us to draw on six (or sixty!) concepts at once. A poem must have language, rhythm, form, line breaks, music, and meaning—all at once. But we can't convey this to children all at once. So far in this unit, we have emphasized form and language over content. Today changes this.

We could have simply told children to choose their topics without giving them instruction on this, but we worried that if given no instruction, children would go toward what they felt were poetic topics (spring, flowers, love).

"I could write a zillion poems and stories about Katie, but I need to zoom in on one small thing—a moment or an object or image that can hold my feeling of admiration—and then I need to see that small thing with poets' eyes, like you've been doing. So watch what I do.

"Let's see. Last weekend we went to the zoo together! That was a really fun experience, and all during it, I kept thinking how much I adore this girl. That's still big, but I'm getting there. I need to zoom in even more. Oh, I know! I bought some food from the little machine so Katie could feed the sheep. At first she was scared to hold her hand toward the sheep's mouth, but then she did it. It was such a sweet moment that somehow captured how special Katie is to me. Now this is getting specific and small.

"If I close my eyes, I can play that moment like a movie in my mind. Katie held her hand out like this." I reenacted how Katie gingerly held her cupped hand toward the sheep. "I can remember how it went, and I can see the image of her hand out like this, and the sheep licking the food off of it." I paused and said, speaking now to the children, "Now I'm ready to write a poem because I have a big topic, a big feeling—how much I adore my niece Katie—and I have something small and specific. I remember how we fed the sheep together."

Show the children a chart on which you've listed some of the strategies you used to generate your idea for a poem.

"Did you see how I did these things?" I revealed what would become an anchor chart. I captured the steps I'd taken, and reminded them of how to get going with their poems once they had a big idea and a small moment that holds that big idea or big feeling.

> ### Strategies Poets Use to Write Poems
>
> - Poets find a big topic that gives them a big feeling.
> - Poets find a small moment, detail, or object that holds the big feeling.
> - Poets look with poets' eyes and see this ordinary thing in a new way.
> - Poets write about it, experimenting with line breaks.

Jane Yolen, an author your students already know and love, wrote a haiku about the small moment in Owl Moon *when her daughter Heidi went looking for owls with her father.*

Owl Moon Haiku
by Jane Yolen

Snowy night, shadows,
What flies silent past the moon?
Pa and I watch owls.

You might wish to share Jane's haiku about Owl Moon, *noting that the big feeling is joy over her husband and daughter's relationship and the small moment is when they go owling together.*

ACTIVE ENGAGEMENT

Help the children coauthor the start of a poem about a shared big feeling.

"Let's try to get started on writing a poem together. Because we're doing this together, we need to think of a big feeling we all have, together. How about this big feeling: loving to listen to a book. Thumbs up if you enjoy being read to!"

A flurry of thumbs went up.

"Now get that big feeling—loving listening to a story—in you right now." I paused to give them time to imagine the pleasure of listening to stories.

"Now close your eyes and think about a small moment or image that you have related to the big feeling of loving to listen to a story. It can be an object—something in the classroom—or it can be the memory of one particular moment. Once you have something in mind, tell your partner what small thing, for *you*, holds the big feeling of loving to listen to stories."

As partners shared, I listened in, hoping to find a partnership whose conversation I wanted to fishbowl. I said in a voiceover, "If you've got something small you want to share that holds this big feeling, will you signal to me? Cup your hand like this if you've found a tiny object or moment that holds a poem, and I'll come listen to you explain it to your partner."

"I've got one," Evette said, holding her hand out as if to show she held the pearl of an idea. When I pulled in to hear her talking to her partner, I heard Evette present what she hoped was the start of a poem. She said: "I love to read."

I reminded her, "That's a big feeling. Remember? It's the one we all started with. What *exactly* do you see or do you recall that goes with that big feeling?" Evette pointed, "That's my place during read-aloud." "That's specific, Evette. There's a poem hiding in that idea. Let's see. Could it start . . . " and I began to record the class poem on chart paper.

> I have a place on the rug
> Where I sit during read-aloud

Evette nodded.

Help children see the concrete detail with fresh eyes.

"Maybe you could think about what happens when you sit there, Evette, and try to see that moment with fresh eyes, like you've been seeing your purplish stone with fresh eyes."

"I sit there and . . . um . . . " Evette hesitated.

We don't in this instance give children a choice over the big topic, following the general rule that we engage children actively in the part of the process we are trying to spotlight at this moment and expedite the other steps of the process by doing them ourselves.

Remember that many children benefit if you translate your big concepts into concrete, physical motions and objects, as we do here. We are picking up on something the children learned in earlier units, which is an especially wise thing to do.

Wyatt, who was still holding his hand gingerly as if it contained the wing of a butterfly, piped in. "Evette, maybe you can say the book opens and the story comes out."

"That's beautiful. You are writing a poem already. 'The book opens. I see . . .' what? Wyatt?"

Wyatt thought, then recited, "'The book opens. I see dragons and stuff."

"You open the book, there is the story, and soon . . . picture it. You are where, exactly?"

Squinching up his face, Wyatt whispered, "Flying on the back of a dragon."

Say the children's own words back to the class as a poem, and extrapolate the lesson you hope writers learn that pertains to another day and text.

"What a poem! Listen," I said and recited their words as a poem, not yet writing it on chart paper but making quick notes to myself to write it up later.

> I have a place on the rug
> where I sit during read-aloud.
> I sit there and the book opens
> and I'm flying on the back of a dragon.

I continued, "Writers, do you see how Wyatt and Evette began with a general feeling of loving to read. Then they zoomed in on the moment when they sit in their reading spots, the book opens, and suddenly they are riding the backs of dragons! What a poem!"

LINK

Remind children of the possibilities they have for writing today.

"Writers, you have so much work to do today! One thing you can do, just like what we did here together, is to find the big topics, the big feelings, in your own lives. You can think of a big feeling you have." I pointed to the first item on the anchor chart. "Then you can find the small moment, detail, or object that holds that big feeling." Again I located my suggestion on the chart. "Then what?" I asked, and children piped in, referencing the remaining bullets on the chart. I nodded. "So you can write new poems that do all these things. You can also reread your existing poems, deciding whether you can revise them so they do all these things. *And* you have a treasure chest full of possible poems. So many choices! When you have a plan for what you want to do today, leave the meeting area and get started!"

Telling children that poets choose a big feeling and then locate that big feeling in something small feels impossibly complex. But when you scaffold children as we do here, the process is not so difficult. This is an example of the teaching method of guided practice. Wyatt is actively doing something—generating a poem—and we use lean prompts to carry him along through the process. In this way, we act almost as training wheels, allowing Wyatt to do something with our support that he couldn't yet do alone.

Our scaffolding has made a world of difference. Wyatt couldn't have written this without our help. That's okay if Wyatt and his classmates learn from this in ways that allow them to write more effectively another day, on another poem.

Balancing Responsive Teaching with Things You Know You Want to Teach

CONFERRING IS OFTEN A BALANCING ACT between noticing and supporting students with the work they are doing, and guiding students into learning that you already have in mind. We often end up doing both kinds of work during one writing session. For example, knowing that you want to bring editing work in as a through-line rather than as something tacked on the end, you could gather a group of students for whom today's minilesson was a breeze, teaching them to bring an editing lens in earlier to their writing process.

While we typically teach more heavily into editing at the end of the writing process, as part of preparing writing for publication, children need to internalize conventions and editing strategies and to use them with increasing automaticity, so that third-graders are not editing for the same conventions as first- and second-graders. Rather than waiting for the end of a unit and editing only what they choose to publish, they can do a quick edit after every day's writing. This will be an invaluable habit to take with them into third grade when they are introduced to the new tool of writers' notebooks. Showing them some simple professional editing marks can pique their interest and take it from being a fun activity to a real habit. Children who see editing as part of writing rather than as a big nuisance can more seamlessly edit as they revise. You can get this kind of work going in your classroom by gathering small groups of children who are ready for it.

On the other hand, you'll absolutely want to be responsive to what comes up as you talk with individuals. In this instance, I knew that Maddie had begun to revise a personal narrative she had written during an earlier unit by turning it into a poem. Pointing out the similarities between focused small moment narratives and poems may inspire students to try reworking their own personal narratives as poems—or at least making poems about the same meaningful moments they described in personal narratives. (Later in the unit, this idea of "story poems" comes up as part of a minilesson about structure, but you may decide to support students' experimentation now in the context of conferences and small groups. One of these student story poems might serve as a strong model for your future minilesson.)

MID-WORKSHOP TEACHING
Reading Our Poems Aloud with Music in Our Voice

"Poets, eyes up here for a minute. I have to tell you, the best part of my day is at the end of it, when I get to curl up on my couch and read through your folders. I get goose bumps over what you have been writing. But poems are meant to be read aloud, and I have noticed that sometimes when you are reading your poetry to your partners, you don't have the music in your voice. You sound a little bit like robot readers. You have worked so hard to give your poems music, it is important that the music comes through in your reading. This made me think that we all need more time to read our poems out loud. We need to listen to the music we are writing into our poems so we don't accidentally read them like robots!

"Get together with your partners. Partner 2 goes first. Look over your poem before you read it so you have it in your heart and you are ready. Then your job is to read your poem aloud with the exact music you want it to have. Read it once, then let there be silence. Then read it again. Afterward, your job, Partner 1, will be to tell Partner 2 what his or her poem made you feel. Then you can switch roles."

Maddie's original story was about the night her baby sister, Isabel, was born, and I remembered well the vivid and poignant images she'd included. I knew Maddie would have no trouble rewriting the lines so her text *looked* more like a poem. She had done this easily and on her own before I approached.

(continues)

We went to the pizza shop before Isabel was born
In the evening
We went there
We got dough
And cheese
When we got home we made a tiny pizza
My mom had a piece and my dad had two

This was one of those moments in which I have to remind myself that my job is to teach the writer, not the writing. The poem belonged to Maddie. As much as I wanted to remind her of all the beautiful images contained in her original story, I knew I had to research to find *her* intentions for this piece. After some conversation, it became clear that Maddie hadn't thought much beyond the idea of making her poem *look* like a poem. She was thinking not of conveying deep meaning, but of faithfully recording events. The line breaks were purely incidental.

I said, "Can I ask you what you hope for your poem? I mean, what do you want people to know or think about when they read it?" I looked at her expectantly.

"I don't know. I just started writing it out of my memory, I wanted people to know what it all looked like."

"Maddie, that's so great. You make it easy for people to visualize what was happening that evening. I want to teach you right now that when writers revise stories into poems, poets *do* make poetry decisions about images, as you did, but there's something else they do even before that: they think about the *meaning*, the big reason it deserves to be a poem, and they make sure the way they write their poem supports that meaning. In today's minilesson we talked about having a big, strong feeling and connecting it to something small. When poets revise, turning a story into a poem like you are doing, they make sure that the stuff they add is still connected to the big feeling of the poem. What *is* the big feeling you want to get across from that night?"

"I guess . . . amazed. I was amazed that she was finally here, and I got to see her when she was still so new."

"Okay, and what is the small image or moment that holds that amazement for you?"

"Ohhh. It's when she was finally born and she was all shiny. She still had some slippery stuff on her. I was holding her for the first time, and I looked in her eyes and she was smiling."

"Wow, Maddie. Wow. You have two great elements of your poem right there. Is the having pizza part you added also connected to the big feeling you just talked about so beautifully?"

"I guess not. I could take it off. But I think waiting for the baby is important because I was waiting and waiting for her to come out!"

I watched for a moment as she got started. After a few lines, I felt ready to leave her to it, so I stopped her to briefly recap our work. "Maddie, before I leave you to work, remember that poets think about connecting the images they add when they revise to the big feeling that the poem is about—just like you're doing with the images you are adding. Ones that don't fit, like the pizza stuff, can be taken out. I'll come check on you again in a bit."

Waiting
For the baby
Mom took lots of walks
One day
The midwife came
Daddy tried to wake me
I was fast
Asleep
The baby came out
I finally woke up
She was crying
I got to hold her. She was
Soft, wet, slippery
With grease and blood
All over her
We looked in each other's eyes
She was smiling at me
Her name was Isabel.

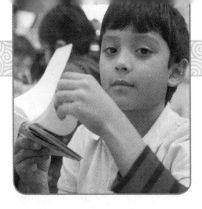

Living Our Lives as Poets

Tiny Topics Notepads

Remind children that they are poets throughout the day, and recruit them to live in ways that let them find poems. Share Naomi Nye's poem "Valentine for Ernest Mann."

"Poets, I want to remind you that you aren't poets for just one hour during the writing workshop. You are poets all day long. When you head home today, you will be traveling home as a poet, entering your home as a poet, talking with someone at home as a poet, and going to sleep as a poet.

"To write poems during our workshop time, you need to follow the advice of Naomi Nye. Remember earlier this year, we read her poem 'Valentine for Ernest Mann'?

"Remember how a child asked her, 'How do you make a poem?' and she answered":

> Valentine for Ernest Mann (excerpt)
> by Naomi Nye
>
> *You can't order a poem like you order a taco.*
> *Walk up to the counter, say, "I'll take two"*
> *and expect it to be handed back to you*
> *on a shiny plate.*
>
> *Still, I like your spirit.*
> *Anyone who says, "Here's my address,*
> *write me a poem," deserves something in reply.*
> *So I'll tell you a secret instead:*
> *poems hide. In the bottoms of our shoes,*
> *they are sleeping. They are the shadows*
> *drifting across the ceiling the moment*
> *before we wake up. What we have to do*
> *is live in a way that lets us find them.*

"Today and every day from now on, I hope you, like Naomi Nye, live in a way that lets you find poems."

Remind children of the Tiny Topics notepads they kept earlier in the year, and suggest they revive these as places to record seeds of poems.

"Remember that earlier this year, when you learned to write from Jane Yolen and Angela Johnson, you kept Tiny Topics notepads? If you were at home or at recess and you saw something tiny, something important that you knew you'd want to remember, you jotted it in your Tiny Topics notepad. I think you need to begin to do that again, only this time you'll observe the details of your life (like shadows that drift across your ceiling or a bird way up in the sky) that could become poems. Write those down, and tomorrow in school, you can look at them like you've been looking at the shells and feathers."

Give out the notepads, and remind the children to pay attention to the poems hiding in their lives.

"So I'm giving you your Tiny Topics notepads—and tonight, remember to follow Naomi Nye's advice and live in a way that lets you find poems. Pay attention. Notice the shadows drifting across the ceiling just after you wake up and all the other poems hiding in your life. Bring your Tiny Topics notepads with you to writing workshop tomorrow."

Just as the teaching in second grade builds upon what students have already learned, so does it lay foundations upon which future teaching will build. The Tiny Topics notepads foreshadow an important tool in the upper-grade writing workshop. Next year, students will keep writer's notebooks and learn about "mining" their entries for important bits of writing. By using this tool now, I am creating schema that future teachers can build upon.

Session 4

Poets Find Poems in the Strong Feelings and Concrete Details of Life

S ESSION 3 ENDED WITH CHILDREN receiving Tiny Topics notepads and being encouraged to follow Naomi Nye's wise advice to live in ways that let them find poems. The goal was that they would come to school today with snippets of their lives captured in key words and phrases—with the hope that this would provide them with topics enough for a few days of writing.

Today's minilesson again emphasizes the idea that poetry is everywhere, and it again conveys that poets mine their notebooks (and their lives) for ideas that contain both strong feelings and concrete details. You'll teach students to peruse their Tiny Topics notepads to choose one or two of their jottings to make into poems—jottings that contain both strong feelings and concrete details. The deeper purpose of the minilesson is to simply remind students that poems are grown from both strong feelings and concrete details. This is a big message, which is why we return to it again in today's session.

Of course, poems come from lots of places. You may think it reductive to insist that students link big feelings and concrete details. We agree that some poets may simply revel in a sensory detail and enjoy finding the words and the form to capture that detail on the page. It's hard not to over simplify from time to time when teaching very young children concepts as complex as these. When we simplify concepts to teach them in strong, decisive ways, the truth is that we do end up reducing the complexity and variety of a topic. Rest assured, however, that concepts will be added to, filled out, and even contradicted as students grow and are exposed to more and more.

Today, as you teach this minilesson, be sure to assess whether you think your children have really heard and taken in the notion that most poems carry big meanings, and do so by grounding those meanings in gritty, specific details.

IN THIS SESSION, you'll teach students that poets are always on the lookout for poems, mining their notebooks and their lives for ideas that have both strong feelings and concrete details.

GETTING READY

✔ Tiny Topics notepads (see Connection and Active Engagement)

✔ Chart paper and marker (see Teaching)

✔ "Strategies Poets Use to Write Poems" chart from Session 3

✔ Your own Tiny Topics notepad to demonstrate mining it for ideas for poems (see Teaching)

✔ Because students will be sharing and celebrating their poems during the next session's share, you may decide to invite an audience. You'll want to prepare for this ahead of time by inviting another class or whomever you choose to invite (see Share).

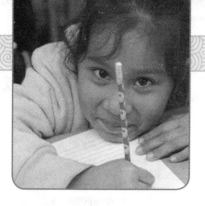

Poets Find Poems in the Strong Feelings and Concrete Details of Life

CONNECTION

Admire the way children have jotted down notes that promise to become poems—and tell them you'll soon teach them to sift through these and make decisions.

"I had such fun this morning listening to ideas you collected in your Tiny Topics notepads. David wrote about looking at different kinds of flowers on the way to school. Abe wrote that you can see trash on the ground, and if you look at it in a special way, you can see that it is really pretty. He's got me thinking that something can be treasure or trash, depending on how you look at it.

"This morning, sifting through the ideas you'd collected, many of you asked me and each other, 'Is this a good idea for a poem?' That's a wise question. Today and often in your life, you'll need to sift through observations and notes and think, 'Okay, is something here waiting to become a great poem?' I'm going to show you how you can read through your notes and make that decision for yourself, instead of asking me.

"Remember when we talked about a few things that go into making a poem? First, poets look at ordinary things in fresh new ways and find words to capture what they see. Second, poets decide how their poems should sound when they are read aloud; they lay the words out on the page to capture that sound, that music.

"And yesterday I told you that when poets want to come up with a topic for a poem, they let their hearts and minds be filled with a big feeling or idea. Then they think about what small thing holds that big feeling, that meaning. Let me say it another way. The subject of a poem has to matter to the poet. It has to give the poet a strong feeling. *Also,* the poem needs to be about a specific moment, object, or memory that holds that big feeling.

"Poems are everywhere, and you have started doing the wonderful work of paying attention and jotting notes to yourselves in your Tiny Topics notepads to help you remember when a poem has gone flying by. Now it's time to make use of those jottings!"

The morning "please do" activity had been to share Tiny Topics notepads with partners and to comment on one another's ideas. As children did this, I circulated and listened in, gathering ideas for the minilesson. A couple of students had forgotten to bring their notepads back to school. I asked these students to jot anything they remembered from their Tiny Topics notepads onto paper while others shared.

Of course, you will want to substitute your children's names and the specifics of what they have said to you. When you do this, make a point of shining a spotlight on students who might not usually be referred to as a mentor for the rest of the class.

When I refer to students' prior learning, I don't generalize and say, "We've been studying poetry." That wouldn't be news to any of them! Instead, I mention specific concepts from previous lessons that will apply to the current one.

✤ Name the teaching point.

"Today I want to teach you that before starting a new poem, poets often review their jotted poem ideas, asking themselves, 'Does this idea contain both strong feelings and concrete details?' and then they start new poems based on ideas that contain both of those elements."

I quickly jotted those two guiding questions onto a piece of chart paper.

TEACHING

Remind children of strategies they have learned for crafting poems.

"Let's look again at our chart of strategies poets use when they begin crafting poems."

> ### Strategies Poets Use to Write Poems
>
> - Poets find a big topic that gives them a big feeling.
> - Poets find a small moment, detail, or object that holds the big feeling.
> - Poets look with poets' eyes and see this ordinary thing in a new way.
> - Poets write about it, experimenting with line breaks.

"Right now I'm going to focus on the first two of these as I reread the jottings in my Tiny Topics notepad."

Demonstrate reading jottings from your Tiny Topics notepad. Think aloud as you examine your notes for both strong feelings and concrete details.

I pulled out my Tiny Topics notepad and opened it. "Our notepads can be like a gold mine, filled with treasure. I know there is gold in my notepad, but not everything in here is gold. Let me show you how I can 'mine' my notepad, looking for the treasure of an idea that could become a poem. Okay, here on this page it says, 'Ginger was slurping up her water.' Now I'm going to ask those two questions. 'Does this give me a strong feeling?' Well, no, it doesn't. Not today, anyway. Maybe it will another day, but not today. I don't even have to ask the second question, since the answer to the first one was 'no.'

"Okay, here's another one. 'I love pizza so much!' If I ask the first question again, the answer is definitely 'yes,' so now I should ask the second question. 'Have I found a specific moment or detail or object that holds that feeling for me?' Hmm. No, I really haven't, have I? This is just a big ol' feeling with no image. Okay, let me keep mining. Wow! It's not easy to find treasure!

This list won't become an anchor chart; it may not even live past today's session. However, I wanted students to be able to refer back to these questions as needed during their independent work time.

For any unit and for any writing workshop, a specialized language emerges, and that is lovely. Let yourself return to a few words often so your students internalize them.

Throughout this minilesson and the unit there are phrases we use often.
- *Poets' eyes*
- *Topics that give a big feeling*
- *See the world like poets do*
- *Look at the world closely and carefully*
- *Small objects and details that hold big feelings*
- *The music of poetry*

I want to imply that if an idea is not calling out to me today, I need not cross it off my list forever. I might return to it another day with different feelings.

"Oh, here we go. 'A pansy is growing out of the crack in the sidewalk.' I do have a strong feeling about this, because I'm so amazed by how such a delicate little flower pushes itself up through the dirty, hard sidewalk. Let me check in with the second question . . . yep, this is a specific moment or detail or object that holds that feeling for me. Now I have mined my notebook and found an idea that could become a poem. I'm going to put a big circle around it."

Debrief, reiterating the two questions that will help children decide if an idea could become a poem.

"You just saw me read through my Tiny Topics notepad, mining it for ideas that could become poems. I did this by asking two important questions about each idea I had jotted down in there. If the answer to both questions is 'yes,' I know it is an idea that could become a poem."

ACTIVE ENGAGEMENT

Invite the children to mine their notepads, asking themselves, "Does this give me a big, strong feeling?" and "Have I found a specific moment or detail or object that holds that feeling for me?"

"Now it's your turn to try it. Go ahead and open your Tiny Topics notepads to the last entry you wrote." I referred to the questions I'd jotted down. "Look at what you wrote, and ask yourself, 'Does this give me a big, strong feeling?' If it does, then ask, 'Have I found a small object or a small moment or a detail that holds the feeling?'" I gave them a moment to read and think. "Tell your partner what you wrote, and talk over if it is both big and small enough to make a poem." After giving students a few minutes to turn and talk, I called the group back together and solicited a few students to share.

Thomas said, "Well, I love insects, and I wrote about how a grasshopper's tummy is musical and its knees have ears."

Alex said, "I love recess, so my feeling is big, but I didn't find a small moment or object to go with my feeling. But right now I just thought of one! When we look out the classroom window, and it's not recess, the monkey bars look too empty."

"Show me a thumb if you realized that your idea wasn't ready to become a poem, at least not yet. Wow, look around at how many people made that important realization! We just tried this quickly with one idea, so now you know how to keep letting these questions guide you as you decide which ideas could become poems. Show me a thumb if you decided that last entry can become a poem. Great! Either way, you now have a strategy for making the decision without having to ask me or anyone else! You are the boss of your own writing, right?"

So far in this unit, you've probably given children six different examples of writers who use a concrete detail to convey a strong feeling. Children will learn more from examples than from instructions.

Looking out of a window, watching a grandmother cook, taking a stream hike—each of these might invite a poem. Kristine O'Connell George explains, "Most of my poems seem to happen when I spend quiet, daydreamy time with something I love. Watching. Looking. Wondering."

LINK

Briefly restate today's teaching before sending children off to write.

"I know that today many of you will start by rereading the jotted notes you have been keeping in your Tiny Topics note-pads. As you do, remember that," and here I essentially read from the anchor chart with a touch of added commentary, "poets find a big topic that gives a big feeling. Poets don't just put these feelings on the paper. Instead, they find a tiny object or detail or moment—like feeding the sheep or being woken up by the lick of a cat—that holds the big feeling. So if you are writing a poem that captures anger, you have to think of a moment or an object that holds your anger. If you are writing about worry, you have to have an object or a moment that holds your worry. If you are writing about your pride at baseball games, you need to zoom in on an object or detail or moment that holds your pride. As you look through your tiny topics notebooks for ideas for your next poems, keep all of that in mind!

"Also, some of you may want to not just mine your Tiny Topics notepads for ideas, you might also want to mine your writing folders! Take a look at some of the observations you made or poems you started. Do any of those hold a big, strong feeling captured in a small moment? If so, that's another idea for a poem or maybe it's a poem you want to revise. Okay, off you go!"

I deliberately choose a variety of feelings to ensure that students know that they too can write poems influenced by a variety of feelings. Often students choose to write about love—and, of course, we know that there are so many more feelings and subtle varieties of feelings that can be the foundation of poems.

Finding and Revising Treasures in Discarded Drafts

A S STUDENTS MINE THEIR TINY TOPICS NOTEPADS, looking for jottings that hold big feelings in small moments, details, or objects, you may find that some children zip past all their entries and come up empty-handed. This may also be the case for children who are trying to decide which poems are worth revising. That is, your teaching today may have inadvertently unhinged some children.

You'll want to confer with these kids or pull a small group if you have a handful that fall into this category. Then you'll need to do a little tightrope act; on the one hand, you'll want to uphold the day's teaching. On the other, you'll need to undo it just a bit to be sure that these kids don't leave the workshop feeling like they have nothing worth writing.

You might say to them, "I pulled you together because you are having the same problem. When you searched your Tiny Topics notepads, trying to decide which ideas give you a strong feeling *and* are anchored in a small object or moment, or in some cases, when you searched your folders, trying to pick which poems are worth revising, you came up empty-handed. I thought to myself, 'How can this be? These children have great writing ideas!' Then I thought it might help you to hear about a trick poets have up their sleeves for when they struggle to find inspiration in their work. Poets know that very often, hiding in the midst of a notebook of ideas, or a folder of poems that don't yet grab hold, is a single line or image that could be the seed of a really great poem. They may have passed it by in their haste, so they give their discarded ideas a second look, with extra-discerning poets' eyes. Annie Dillard writes about this in *The Writing Life*. She says, 'It is handed to you, but only if you look for it . . . One line of a poem, the poet said—only one line, but Thank God for that one line—drops from the ceiling.'"

You could then ask the children in the group to revisit their Tiny Topics notepads or their folders, paying special attention this time to a search for just one line or fragment of an idea that stands out. It might be that the line gives them a big feeling or that it feels especially fresh. You could suggest that children circle that line and then "lift" it out and onto a fresh new page. They can then begin a whole new poem around that one bit.

If you give children a few minutes to work as they sit together in the small group, you can watch for children who seem to be having success and find out what they have done. Then you could share whatever you discover. Sarah, for example, had written an entry called "Moms."

It went like this (see Figure 4–1).

MID-WORKSHOP TEACHING
You Can All Be Writing Teachers for Each Other

"Remember earlier this year when I told you that there's not just one writing teacher in this room, but there are twenty-eight of us? Well, there's not just one poetry teacher in this room, either! You can each be a poetry teacher. We learned early on how to ask for and offer help, and that still applies in this unit of study. Remember that if you need help, your partner can give you suggestions.

"Partners, when you are asked to help, to be a writing teacher, your job is to listen to the poem carefully, and also listen to the poet. Instead of just saying what you would do if this was your poem, try to find out what *the poet* wants to do with his or her poem, and then try to help. Use the 'Strategies Poets Use to Write Poems' chart to help each other."

Figure 4-1 (handwritten)

```
moms
moms are grate
everyone has a mom
yor moms gona see you
tonight but my mom comes
home late.
but
my moms
still grate!
```

FIG. 4–1 Sarah finds a "drop from the ceiling" line in her poem.

Moms (typeset)

Moms are great
everyone has a mom
your mom's gonna see you
tonight but my mom comes
home late
but
my mom's
still great!

Figure 4-2 (handwritten)

```
My mom comes home
Beep! beep!
my mom walks throo the
door and yells hello
I dash upstars
my mom looks tiyerd
she eas dinner
then she lise on the
couch and wachis tv
mabby she was
wrieing prochrms?
mabby she was
reading pappers?
```

```
Maybe the tranes worint runing
so well but I'm still happy that my
mom came home!
```

sarah

FIG. 4–2 Sarah's revised poem

My Mom Comes Home Late (typeset)

Beep! Beep!
My mom walks through the
door and yells hello.
I dash upstairs
my mom looks tired
she eats dinner
then she lies on the
couch and watches TV
Maybe she was
writing programs?
Maybe she was
reading papers?
Maybe the trains weren't
running
so well but I'm still happy
that my
mom came home!

I said to the small group, "The first time Sarah read this, she didn't see anything worth salvaging. But just now, Sarah realized that she does have one favorite line in this poem. The line 'But my mom comes home late' is one of those 'drops from the ceiling' lines. She said that image was important and that there was a big feeling in it that wasn't in the rest of the poem. Look at what she did next." I held up a piece of paper with just that phrase written at the top. "She lifted that line right off of the page and wrote it onto this page! She thought, 'I can make a new poem out of it.' Look at what Sarah wrote!" (See Figure 4–2.)

I continued explaining to the group the step-by-step procedure that Sarah did. "She explained that she read through poems in her 'no' pile, asking herself, 'Does this poem have any 'drop from the ceiling' lines? She then thought about each line as she read." I held up the original poem. "When she found one that gave her a big feeling, she circled it and wrote it at the top of a fresh piece of paper, like this one." I held up that piece of paper. "Then she made it into a new poem!" And I held up the final poem.

As you work with children like Sarah, either in conferences or in small groups, you may need to guide them toward lines that hold potential. Sometimes they won't realize when they have written something powerful, which evokes emotion, or created an image that feels especially novel. Of course, if a child has written mostly clichéd, pedestrian lines, you may instead need to work with him to come up with something that feels a bit more unique to his experience, his imagination, and his way of looking at and writing about the world.

Choosing and Preparing Poems to Celebrate

Let poets know that soon they will be choosing a poem for a mini-publishing celebration. Remind them that it is important to think about their audience.

"Poets, I've been thinking that we might invite other people from the school to our room to hear some of the poems you have written—another class. That means that each one of you has an important job to do: you need to think, of all the poems you've written so far, which one or two deserve to get an audience? Ask yourself, 'Does this poem have fresh images that readers will enjoy? Does it have music that readers will want to hear? Does it hold special meaning?'

"Take just a minute to select one or two of your poems to publish. Once you have the selected poems in hand, give me a thumbs up."

Ask students to read their chosen poems to each other and to give each other feedback about what is working and what is not working.

I waited until many children had given me the signal and then said, "Partner 1, in just a minute, you will read a poem that you selected to Partner 2, using your best performing poet's voice. After you read your poem, listen to your partner's response (even if you have two poems to share, after you read one, talk about it). Partner 2, notice what you especially like in Partner 1's poem; maybe you like a particular image or the music in the poem. Notice, also, what *isn't* yet working. Does a line sound bumpy? Are you confused? Be ready to talk about specific examples."

If you can arrange for another class to visit, that will ramp up your children's energy. But there are many smaller ways to do that as well. Might one or two children read their poems to younger children each morning, or might you devote a bulletin board to sharing students' poetry?

Editing Poetry

YOUR CHILDREN WILL EACH HAVE A POEM or two that they're determined to share today. The prospect of publication will mean your children will come to the writing workshop with a renewed energy to work. Tap into this! Remind them that now they'll want to reread each poem, asking, "Is this my best?"

Of course, editing won't be new for your students. They have a large repertoire of strategies for editing that they learned throughout the year as they edited their narratives, lab reports, and opinion pieces. You'll remind them to use all these strategies. Poems are short, and this makes it easy for young writers to scrutinize every word. They'll do this, checking their spelling, along with other conventions. You can still expect spelling to be grade appropriate. Every word won't be correctly spelled, but it is helpful to convey to children that they should be increasingly aware of words that just don't quite "look right," even in instances when they may not be sure what exactly is wrong with the way a word has been spelled.

In today's session, you'll teach children to focus on the words that seem not quite right. You'll show your youngsters that it is effective to try spelling those words two or three different ways, circling the attempt that seems best. Children can also consult resources (books in which a word appears, a children's dictionary, a friend) to learn the correct spelling. You'll emphasize the importance of comparing and contrasting the child's best effort and the conventional spelling not only so that children can arrive at the correct spelling, but so they can also learn from this process.

This minilesson assumes that students have located words in dictionaries before now. If this is very new to your youngsters, you'll want to give some introduction to this before continuing with the minilesson, or you'll modify the minilesson.

Because of its condensed nature, poetry is a perfect genre to teach children the importance of closely scrutinizing their writing to make sure each word is spelled accurately. Today you'll teach children to reread with pen in hand, carefully checking each word and then doing everything possible to fix words that require more attention.

IN THIS SESSION, you'll teach students that poets edit their poems, paying close attention to spelling. Young poets circle words that look incorrectly spelled and draw on strategies to fix these.

GETTING READY

- ✔ A model poem written on chart paper with some spelling errors (see Teaching)

- ✔ Dictionaries for teacher modeling and student use (see Teaching and Link)

- ✔ "Give It a Shot!" spelling chart, with columns titled "First Try," "Second Try," and "Dictionary" (see Teaching)

- ✔ Clipboards, paper, and pencils, for students to create their own "Give It a Shot!" charts to practice spelling different words (see Active Engagement)

- ✔ "Language Conventions" portion of the Opinion Writing Checklist, Grade 2, displayed on a chart and enough copies for each student. (see Link)

- ✔ Students will need to have chosen a poem or two to share today. You may want to have invited another class for the end of workshop share time, to have an audience for your mini-celebration.

Editing Poetry

CONNECTION

Remind children that to prepare their poems to share, they will need to edit their poems carefully.

"It won't be long before you are able to publish your poems. I have to tell you, though, I heard the oddest rumor this morning. I heard there are some kids in this school who think poets don't edit poetry!" I gasped and put my hand to my mouth, pantomiming utter shock. "Of course, it is true that there are some poets who make the decision to use all lowercase letters—no capitals at all. And poets sometimes make the decision to write with just words or phrases instead of whole sentences. But poets think long and hard before doing something like that, and they do it for special reasons, not just because they are sloppy!

"It is absolutely not the case that a poet would just *not care* about a comma, a period, a quotation mark, or a spelling. Because here's the thing about poetry: every single mark matters. In fact, poets spend more time than other writers thinking about every single mark and every single spelling because poems are meant to be read aloud."

Point out that children have reached for words they've never tried to spell before, and because of this, they'll need to pay careful attention to how they've spelled these words.

"Because poems need the very best words possible, many of you have used words in your poems that you've never written before. You've searched the world for the exactly right words, and sometimes they are really odd, cool words that you may not have used in any other piece of writing.

"If you are not exactly sure whether you spelled some of those words right, remember that the brain is a powerful observer! It may not know how to spell a word, but it knows whether a word on your paper looks right or looks wrong. Careful writers can use this to help them spell."

You should expect a lot of energy as today's writing workshop approaches. Students know the celebration is right around the corner and that their last step is to edit and illustrate their poems. You'll want to harness this energy for editing. Be absolutely sure that your children don't carry the mistaken notion that "conventions don't matter in poetry."

Demonstrate that you value risk taking, something that students can control. It is wise to focus compliments on what students can control, not on what comes naturally to them. As this lesson continues, you will see that such respect for risk taking is balanced by a respect for careful editing habits.

✦ **Name the teaching point.**

"Today I want to teach you that when writers are trying to spell words so people can read their writing, they look at each word they've written and ask, 'Does that look right? Look wrong?' When you find a word that doesn't look right, it can help to spell that word a few different ways, looking to see if one looks right."

TEACHING

Pretend to be a student and recruit the class to join you in checking whether the words in your poem look right or not, in which case you'll circle them (and return to them later).

"I'm going to pretend to be an eight-year-old poet named Maria." Getting into character, I said, "Will you help me check my words? I want to be sure each one looks right. I definitely want people to be able to read my poem." I turned the chart paper to reveal a poem that had several spelling errors. The first line was written like this.

> Delicate and frageil

I read the first line aloud and then said, "*Delicate*. That looks right to me. I think that's okay. I don't need to even think about *and*. Now *frageil*. Hmm. That does not look right to me." I circled it and went on in this manner through the next two lines, circling also the words *climd* and *climbes*.

> They climd
> She climbes up the grassy hill

Demonstrate spelling each word two different ways, highlighting that you use what you know about spelling patterns to help.

"Now I have three words circled. I'm going to start with *frageil*. I'm pretty sure the *fra* part is good. That's what writers do, they think which part of the word looks right, so let me think about spelling the second part. I think it ends in a silent *e*. Okay, so maybe it is *frajile* or maybe it is *fragile*. I'm going to write these up here on the chart.

"I don't think I need to try a third way. One of these is already looking right to me. I could double-check with the dictionary, if I wanted to." I picked up a copy of our class dictionary and talked through the process of finding the word. "Here it is! Yes, it is just as I thought! *f-r-a-g-i-l-e*. I'll circle it.

"Now, let's try the same process with my next word, *climd*. I will try out different spellings. As I do that, think about which spelling looks right to you." I repeated the process with *climd* but this time did not arrive at a correct spelling. My two attempts were *climed* and *climbd*. This time, instead of checking the dictionary, I asked a friend for help, stressing that there are a variety of ways to get help. I added the correct spelling to my list and circled it. When I was done, my chart looked like this.

Why pretend to be an eight-year-old? Because it's more honest than acting as if you, as an adult, can't spell, and children value honesty. They know that you are not likely to have difficulty spelling the words in these poems. But pretending to be an eight-year-old allows you to demonstrate the challenges your students might actually face, in a way that they can believe. Besides, it's fun!

You could decide to move on to the active engagement at this point. You'll always want to judge what your kids are game for.

Give It a Shot! Spelling Chart

First Try | Second Try | Dictionary/Friend
frajile | (fragile) |
climed | climbd | (climbed)
climes | (climbs) |

ACTIVE ENGAGEMENT

Ask the class to look at the next two lines of your poem as carefully as you looked at the first ones, finding any words that don't look quite right to them.

"Now it's your turn to try this strategy! Pull out your clipboards and draw two vertical lines to make your own 'Give It a Shot!' chart, with three columns." I did this as I spoke. "We'll look at the next two lines of my poem together. I'll read. Will you show me a thumb when a word doesn't look quite right to you?"

> Hourses
>   With beutiful silky maines

"Okay, so we've circled *hourses, beutiful,* and *maines.* I saw some of you put a thumb up for the word *silky,* but since a majority of you say it definitely looks right, we'll leave it as is. In the first two columns of your paper, try each of those words in two different ways."

As children worked, I coached. "Think about everything you know about how letters, sounds, syllables, and words work." A bit later, I said, "If you know the word, then just write what you know." I then asked them to turn and talk, discussing their attempts with their partners.

After calling them back together, I said, "I want to hear how you came to the correct spelling for each word."

Khalea said, "Maddie and I both had the same thing for *beautiful,* so we thought it must be the real way." I invited her to come add it to the class chart, which she did. The class agreed that her spelling looked right, and it was indeed the correct spelling.

Sarah said, "*Maines* was hard because there's *main,* like the main idea, and then there's *Maine,* the state, and then this *mane*—on a horse. So a bunch of things looked right. This was one where we needed the dictionary, so we could make sure we had the right *mane.*"

Often in minilessons, the teacher demonstrates for a bit and then passes the baton to children, and they continue where the teacher left off.

As I read, I looked for raised thumbs, noting those children who didn't seem to see anything wrong with any word. There were about four of these students, and I was already mentally compiling a small group.

You ask students to share the process of "how you came to the correct spelling" because this is a replicable process. The actual spelling of horses *is much less important than how a child arrives at a particular spelling. You are teaching both spelling and editing habits today, and your words concerning editing will influence students' drafting work in the days to come.*

I hadn't planned it this way, but since it came up, I displayed our class dictionary on the overhead and let the kids direct me in locating the word, which I then added to the chart.

LINK

Send the children off to edit their own poems, reminding them to use the writing checklist to know what to check for in their writing.

I revealed the "Language Conventions" portion of the Opinion Writing Checklist for Grade 2 we had used in the previous unit.

 "Today we talked about two kinds of resources: making a 'Give It a Shot!' chart and our class dictionaries. Of course, the word wall, any book in the library, and the words written all over our classroom can also be resources. As spellers, you don't yet know every word you might want to write, and using a resource can help you with the ones you don't yet know!

"As you go off, remember that if you are editing, you can use the Language Conventions part of our writing checklist." I pointed to the checklist I had displayed. "I have copies for each of you."

"You'll be sharing your poems at the end of workshop today, so make sure you get your poems ready for readers! Remember to check your capitals, commas, and other punctuation, and remember to spell each word the best you can. Off you go!"

	Language Conventions			
Spelling	To spell a word, I used what I knew about spelling patterns (*tion, er, ly*, etc.). I spelled all of the word wall words correctly and used the word wall to help me figure out how to spell other words.	☐	☐	☐
Punctuation	I used quotation marks to show what characters said. When I used words such as *can't* and *don't*, I put in the apostrophe.	☐	☐	☐

Consider keeping dictionaries at your students' tables or provide each child with small personal dictionaries to keep in their folders. They will be more likely to use a handy resource than one kept across the room.

You'll be aware already that the Writing Pathways *book doesn't contain an assessment tool for poetry. Borrowing the conventions section of the opinion chart is a good idea, however.*

Differentiating Your Editing Support through Small-Group Work

YOU MAY NOTICE THAT CHILDREN NEED DIFFERENTIATED SUPPORT when it comes to editing, which you can provide in small groups.

Today you'll want to take stock of where your kids are—quickly—and then you'll want to put on roller skates to get to as many of them as possible. If you have children who have been absent or for some other reason have yet to really accomplish a lot of writing and revising, you may want to spend some time giving those children quick, efficient help that moves them along a pathway to producing more drafts or toward completing and revising those that are somewhere in the writing process pipeline. That is, don't feel that just because your minilesson highlights editing you necessarily will devote yourself entirely to that.

On the other hand, you will absolutely want to support editing. Presumably it will be especially efficient if you assess your children's work with conventions prior to today's workshop. Which of them are still spelling high-frequency words by sounding them out rather than remembering that these are words they know "by heart" and can spell by memory? If you have a few children who are in that category, you may want to gather them together. You could say to them, "I pulled you guys together because I need to tell you that the four of you are all working too hard! Not really—no one in life can really work too hard—but you are working too hard to stretch out words and listen to the sounds—word solving work—when those are words that you need to know in a snap." You might teach kids that the first job, really, is to be able to think of a word and say, "That's one I should know by heart." or "That's one I need to solve."

Then you might give these children dictionaries or their own word walls or some similar tool that essentially is an assessment-based high-frequency word list. That list can be different for different members of your group. Patricia Cunningham (*Making Words*) has suggested word lists by grade level, and you might direct some of your children toward her first-grade word list for starters (until that is under their belt) and others to the second- or third-grade word list. Perhaps you'll want children to read through the lists and highlight the words that they "sorta, kinda" know. Then it will be important for children to reread their poems, looking for times when they have tried to spell one of those high-frequency words. "When you come to a word like, say, *because* that you know is a word you should know, instead of word solving it, say, 'Wait, I know that word!' and try to get a mental image of it in your mind. Then try to write it. If you need

MID-WORKSHOP TEACHING   Tackling Tricky Vowels

"Poets, eyes up here." I said and waited. "I'm hearing from many of you that when you tackle the hard words, the vowel sounds are the hardest part. I'm not surprised. Did you know that researchers say that the letter *o* makes—get this—sixteen different sounds? So it is often a bit challenging to know how to spell the middles of some of your words.

"I'm proud that some of you are coming up with strategies for tackling this hard part. Abe told me he tried a few different ways to spell a word, and—here's the more important thing—he tried a few different strategies. His word was *bicycle*. First, he broke the word into syllables and reminded himself that he needed one vowel in each syllable. So he came up with a spelling based on that. Then he remembered that it can help to ask, 'Do I know any words that are like this one—words that sound the same?' So he thought about the water cycle we have been studying and tried spelling *cycle* inside the word *bicycle*.

"Would all of you remember that when you come to something tricky, it helps to choose a strategy? Right now, Partner 2, see if you can find a hard word." I left the children a few seconds to do this. "Now, try spelling that hard word to your partner using one strategy—like Abe's syllable strategy—and then using a different strategy. Go!"

After children did this work for a few minutes, I channeled them to remember this as they continued writing and editing.

to do so, find it on your word list, then fix your mind on the word, get it into your mind, and then write it on your paper. That is, don't look at a part of the word, copy it, look at the next part, copy it, and so on."

Of course, there will be other issues that you want to take up during editing. In poetry, few things matter more than using precisely chosen words, so you might work with children on that. Then again, children sometimes think that poems are excuses to write without holding themselves to high standards for meaning making, in which case you'll need to address this. Always, look to see whether there are a few children who could use help tackling similar challenges, and work with them in small groups.

When you lead small groups, you might think for a bit about how the methods of teaching differ based on the children with whom you teach. Your strugglers may need more scaffolds; your especially proficient poets may need more assignments and goal setting. One of the marks of effective group work is that the methods of teaching are not all the same in all your groups.

Celebration

Invite children to share their work with outside readers, celebrating the hard work they've done to get their poems ready to go out into the world.

I called the children to the rug, asking them to bring their edited poems with them. "Poets, we are so lucky today to have 2-107 visiting us today. You've chosen poems that mean a lot to you, you've revised and edited them and practiced reading them, and now it's almost time to read them! 2-107 is waiting outside. Let's invite them in and make them feel welcome, and then each of you will have a chance to read a poem aloud."

Here are a few poems that students read aloud during this mini-celebration (see Figures 5–1, 5–2, 5–3, 5–4, and 5–5).

This is a very simple and quick celebration, easily arranged with a nearby colleague. We don't expect a lot of fanfare here—just an opportunity for poets to share their work, giving them energy to keep writing at this very early stage in the unit and to hit home the fact that poetry is important—worth celebrating, worth integrating into a life. As Erica Jong wrote, "People think they can do without poetry and they can. At least until they fall in love, lose a friend, lose a child, or lose their way in the dark woods of life. People think they can live without poetry, at least until they become fatally ill, have a baby, or fall desperately, madly, in love" (In Their Own Voices, 203).

How did the Water Cycle begined?

Were you one of the first drops?
Did you start the water cycle?
How do you get on clouds?
I want to see your rainbow.

How do you evaporate?
What is it like?
How do you fall on the ground?
Do you like evaporating?
I wish I was a drop.

FIG. 5–1 Evette

How Did the Water Cycle Begin?
by Evette

Were you one of the first drops?
Did you start the water cycle?
Do you like going in circles?
How do you get on clouds?
I want to see your rainbow.

How do you evaporate?
What is it like?
How do you fall on the ground?
Do you like evaporating?
I wish I was a drop.

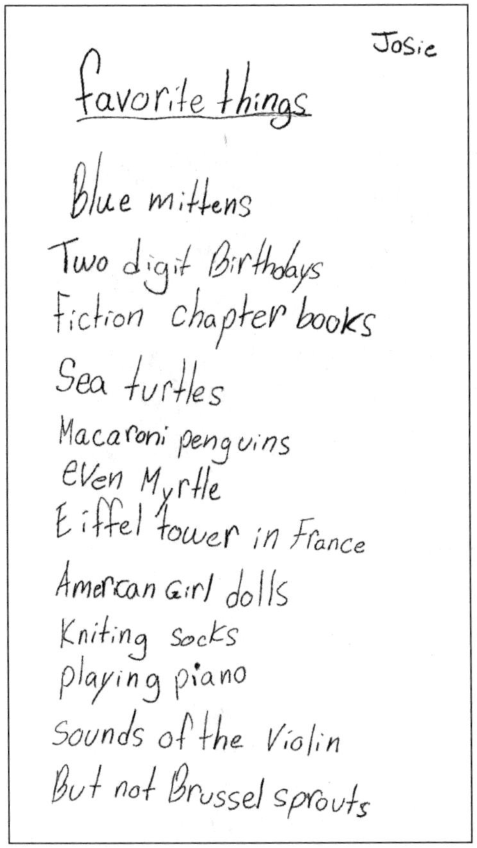
Josie

favorite things

Blue mittens
Two digit Birthdays
Fiction chapter books
Sea turtles
Macaroni penguins
even Myrtle
Eiffel tower in France
American Girl dolls
Kniting socks
playing piano
Sounds of the Violin
But not Brussel sprouts

FIG. 5–2 Josie

favorite things

by Josie

Blue mittens
Two digit birthdays
Fiction chapter books
Sea turtles
Macaroni penguins
even Myrtle
Eiffel tower in France
American Girl dolls
Knitting socks
Playing piano
Sounds of the violin
But not brussel sprouts

Cinnamon Stick!

by Sophia

Cinnamon stick
a rolled up piece of bark.
A brown tube that smells
calm and heavenly.
Like natural sugar just for
sensing with your nose.
Like a mini canoe for
people who are one inch tall.
Sweet and heavenly
I wish I could eat it right
now.
Cinnamon stick
a rolled up piece of bark.

FIG. 5–3 Sophia

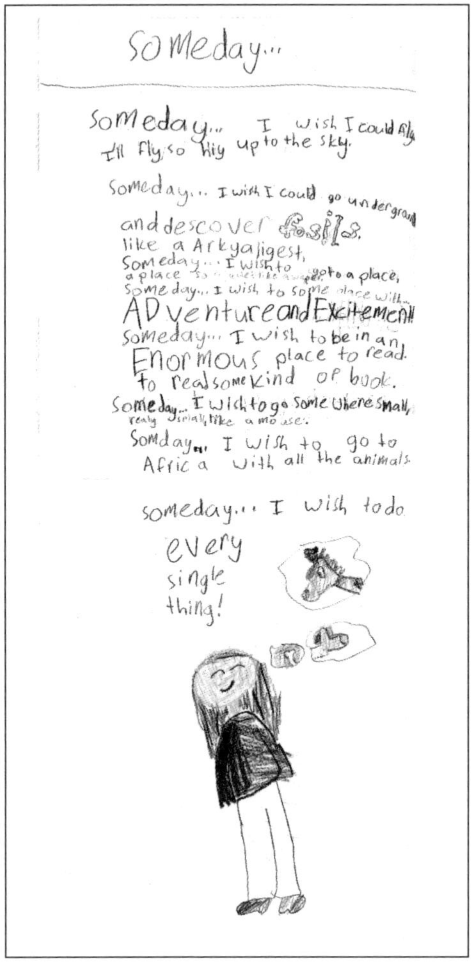

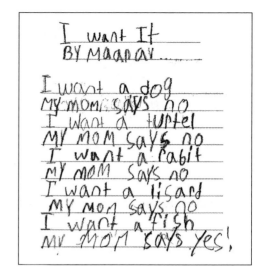

FIG. 5–4 Bergin

Someday . . .

by Bergin

Someday . . . I wish I could fly.
I'll fly so high up to the sky.
Someday . . . I wish I could go underground
and discover fossils
like an archaeologist.
Someday . . . I wish to go to a place
a place so so so quiet like a whisper.
Someday . . . I wish to go someplace with . . .
Adventure and Excitement!
Someday . . . I wish to be in an
Enormous place to read,
to read some kind of book.
Someday . . . I wish to go somewhere small
really small, like a mouse.
Someday . . . I wish to go to
Africa with all the animals.
Someday . . . I wish to do
every
single
thing!

I want It
BY Maanav

I want a dog
My mom says no
I want a turtel
My mom says no
I want a rabit
My mom says no
I want a lisard
My mom says no
I want a fish
My mom says yes!

FIG. 5–5 Maanav

I Want It

by Maanav

I want a dog
My mom says no
I want a turtle
My mom says no
I want a rabbit
My mom says no
I want a lizard
My mom says no
I want a fish
My mom says yes!

Searching for Honest, Precise Words

Language Matters

IN THIS SESSION, you'll teach students that poets think carefully about the words that they choose, searching for precisely the right ones to match what they are trying to say.

GETTING READY

✔ Your own poem with a few imprecise words, enlarged on chart paper (see Teaching)

✔ Chart paper and marker (see Teaching and Active Engagement)

✔ Shared class poem from Session 3, enlarged on chart paper (see Active Engagement)

✔ "Poetry Decisions that Strengthen Meaning" chart (see Link)

✔ Poetry wall for collecting mentor poems and student poem lines (see Mid-Workshop Teaching)

✔ Index cards for students to copy lines from their poems to go on the poetry wall

✔ "Aquarium" by Valerie Worth, enlarged on chart paper (see Share)

✔ "Lullaby" by Kristine O'Connell George, enlarged on chart paper (see Share)

I N BEND I, you introduced children to one way poets make poems: first, poets look at the world in fresh ways, finding words to capture what they see; second, they turn their words into "music," experimenting with line breaks to get the sounds just right. Your students learned, too, that poets write about topics that matter to them. Specifically, they come up with a big feeling or idea, which they then anchor in a small object, moment, or detail.

By now, your students are immersed in the sounds and language of poetry, and they are beginning to grasp how to generate their own poetry topics by asking themselves, "Do I have a strong feeling about this?" and "Have I found a specific moment or detail or object that holds that feeling for me?" They are ready, then, for the work of this second bend, in which you unpack the teaching you laid out in Bend I. Together, you and your students will explore various ways that poets use language and sound to bring yet more meaning and clarity to their writing.

Poetry is an ideal genre for you to teach students the importance of focusing on precise, powerful language. In particular, you can teach children to describe people, places, things, feelings, concepts, thoughts, and actions of all kinds—with an emphasis on pushing beyond generic descriptors. World-class standards suggest that second grade is the perfect age for children to learn to use words such as *quickly* or *sluggishly* to describe actions, and words such as *delicate* or *hefty* to describe objects and things. The standards also expect second-graders to distinguish shades of meaning among closely related action words (e.g., distinguishing between *toss*, *throw*, and *hurl*) and closely related descriptors (e.g., distinguishing between *slender*, *skinny*, and *scrawny*).

Today you'll build off of Session 1's focus on seeing the world in fresh ways to help children think carefully about language choice; specifically, you will help your students learn to clarify the images they see and then to reach for precise words that best convey those images.

Of course, it will be especially important to help children learn that it's possible to describe something with precision without writing a long list of adjectives. Often the most descriptive passages in literature are made with precise detail. Think of Cynthia Rylant describing the house in *The Relatives Came*: "It was hard going to sleep with all that new breathing in the house!" This one image—all that new breathing—calls to mind the many times the house has been brimful of relatives sleeping over—and yet it was written with just a few simple words. Notice there's nothing fancy in this description. Likewise, rather than praising "beautiful" or "exciting" language, you'll advocate for children to reach for words that exactly match what they want to say—words that do the best job of communicating what's in their hearts and minds.

"Poetry is an ideal genre for you to teach students the importance of focusing on precise, powerful language."

In *A Poetry Handbook: A Prose Guide to Understanding and Writing Poetry*, Pulitzer Prize–winning poet Mary Oliver (1994) writes, "The language of the poem is the language of particulars. Without it, poetry might still be wise, but it would surely be pallid. And thin. It is the detailed sensory language incorporating images that gives the poem dash and tenderness. And authenticity." In today's lesson, you will help children to focus on these particulars of life, these scenes. And in learning to see the clarity in such particulars, they will also learn to find clarity and understanding in stories, in information, and in everyday life.

Searching for Honest, Precise Words

CONNECTION

Tell a story about a person who searched for the exactly right words, tried generalities, and settled on a fresh, metaphorical way to describe something.

"Listen to this story. Yesterday my friend Emily called me on her cell phone from the beach. She said, 'I called because there is something so beautiful here, and I wanted to share it with you.' It turned out there were these shells all over the beach that amazed her. She said to me, 'They're little and purpley.'

"I said, 'Emily, I can't picture them! Say a little more about them.' So she said, 'They're tiny purple mussel shells, open, but still connected, and they look like a million purple butterflies flying in the sand.' When she said that, all of a sudden I could see it!

This tiny anecdote is worth studying. What makes it so effective? I think it profits enormously from the image of Emily on the beach with her cell phone in hand; we can see the scene, and there is an urgency that comes with Emily trying to transmit the image of the beautiful shells into the very concrete and constrained cell phone.

"My friend Emily searched for the exactly right words to tell me about the shells. That's what poets do. She was looking at the shells right in front of her, searching for the words that would exactly match what she saw. 'A million purple butterflies, flying in the sand.'

"Poets, for the next week or so, we're going to be learning lots of ways that poets develop the language and music in their poems to make them meaningful and crystal clear."

❖ Name the teaching point.

"What I want to teach you today is that poets think very carefully about the words they choose. They search for the exact, honest words, words that match what they are trying to say. Poets reread their poetry and ask themselves, 'Are these words creating the image that I want?' If not, poets revise."

TEACHING

Use your own poem to model rereading, checking to see if the words match the image you are trying to portray. Walk students through the steps you take to make your language more precise.

"I am going to show you what I mean with a poem that I wrote yesterday about my mom. Watch as I reread it and ask myself, 'Am I saying exactly what I want to say?'" Notice what I do to make my words precisely right because then you can try the same process."

My Mom

In my lunchbox
A frozen juice.
Because it's hot today,
covered in paper
so it won't melt.
How come I never
Ever
See her
Do this?

"Hmm. I did get a big feeling and find a small detail that holds that feeling, but I'm not sure if my words are making the exact image I have in my mind. I'm looking at this word *covered*. I realize it isn't the exact, true word. I'm going to circle it." I drew a circle around the word and turned back to the class. "That was the first step. I reread my poem and asked myself if my words were the exact ones that my image needed. When I found a word that didn't seem to be the right one, I circled it. Now let me show you how I revise it.

"I have an image in my mind, and I want my readers to see what I see. Here comes step 2. I'm going to close my eyes and peek into my lunch box. I see the juice covered in paper. Well, not quite covered, so let me list as many words as I can think of that might more precisely match my image." As I considered a few words, I wrote them on the chart paper beside the circled word. "Let's see. Could it be wrapped? Held? Maybe nestled? Protected? Okay, now I have some choices." I looked at the chart for a few seconds and then said, "Protected. That's definitely the image I am reaching for. The paper seemed to *protect* my juice from the heat. And that's sort of like my mom *protecting* me from the heat. And that was step 3!"

Debrief, listing the replicable steps children can take to use more specific language in their poems.

"Poets, did you see how I went through those three steps so I could find the precise word?" As I listed my steps, I held up a finger for each one. "First, I reread, asking if my words exactly matched my image and circling any that didn't. Then I closed my eyes to see the image in my head and to list other possible words. Finally, I chose the precise word I wanted from the list—the one that best matched my image *and* my meaning. I'm going to hang up this example so you can

---

When you write texts as examples, it's great to make them close to the sort of thing your children could write. The topic and simplicity of this poem makes it a perfect one, and you could revisit it in future minilessons in which you teach the power of detail and of "show, not tell."

It is so important that we teach children to reach for exact, specific, true words rather than for fancy words. You'll notice that we never exalt the advantages of "beautiful words." Instead, we talk up "precise words."

see the process." I added some words and pictures to the chart so that children could refer to it through the rest of the unit if they wanted to try this strategy again.

ACTIVE ENGAGEMENT

Using a class poem, channel students to search for places where more precise words could be added.

"Now I'm going to give you a chance to try this with our poem about read-aloud. Read the poem, thinking about the images. Do you see any parts of the poem that do not convey the image and meaning exactly as you'd like? That's step one. Next, you'll work with your partner to list a few words, or even phrases, that more exactly match your image and meaning."

Read-aloud

I have a place on the rug
Where I sit during read-aloud
I sit there and the book opens
And I'm
    Flying on the back of a dragon
    Riding a motorcycle
    Feeding bugs to a frog
    Winning the blue banner
A story comes out
Another world comes alive
And we are in it

After children read for a minute, the room broke into a buzz. As partners talked, I called out little coaching tips, circulating among them. I reminded children to close their eyes to see the image in their minds and to reach for precise words to describe it. I reminded children to be active listeners, building on each other's ideas rather than just offering their own thoughts or one-upping each other.

Share some of what you heard, highlighting students' ideas about where to add more precise words and circling those places in the poem.

I listened in on the conversations and after a few minutes reconvened the group. "Poets, I heard Khalea say that the book doesn't just *open*, so let's circle that word. I also heard Ramon say that *comes out* doesn't really match his image of what it's like to hear the story, so I'm circling that, too.

"Now we're onto step 3. Close your eyes and remember our read-aloud time. Remember me, opening the book. Remember a great story—maybe *My Father's Dragon* or *Stuart Little*—or any story you choose. Does the book *open* and does the story *come out*? For either, *opens* or *comes out*, see if your image makes you think of other, more precise words."

Collect precise words to replace the circled words.

Soon the class had accumulated a short list for each word and phrase, which I recorded on the chart:

Instead of OPENS, we might write . . .

- pops open
- bursts open
- spreads its wings

Instead of COMES OUT, we might write . . .

- flies to us
- grabs our ears
- fills the room

"As I point to each suggestion, put up a thumb if this is a precise word or phrase that you think describes what is happening during read-aloud." I read through the chart and we arrived at a consensus. "We just did what poets do. We tried to find the exact true words, like Emily did when she saw those shells."

LINK

Remind students that they now have a repertoire of strategies for writing poetry, and invite them to use any of these strategies.

"We've begun to grow a list of strategies poets use as they write poems. Today you can try this one, or you can invent new strategies. Come get me if you invent something new so I can admire what you have done. I'm going to start a chart of all the ways we can strengthen the meaning in our poems."

Poetry Decisions that Strengthen Meaning

Make Meaning with Images
- Use honest, precise words.
- Show, not tell.

Make Meaning with Music
- Pay attention to line breaks.

This list is long enough. One time when Marie Clay toured our reading and writing workshops, she said, "Generally, once a list holds more than three or four items, it ceases to be useful. After a while, the reader of a list should be able to fill in the 'and so on, and so ons.'

Notice that often, minilessons end with you adding a new strategy to children's ongoing repertoire.

Showing, Not Telling

WHEN YOU CONFER AND WORK WITH SMALL GROUPS TODAY, one of the things you'll look for is the degree to which children seem to be transferring what they have learned earlier this year into poetry. For example, you've taught children to include direct quotations, to use domain-specific words, and to write with sensory details. How much of that are they remembering to do now that they are writing poetry? You've taught children to show, not tell, too. Are they bringing those lessons into this unit? If children aren't transferring what they have learned earlier, you'll want to encourage them to do so.

When I drew a chair alongside Ramon, he announced to me, "Well, I like this poem I did yesterday. It's all done. I was just reading it again to check if I like it and I do! So I'm gonna start another poem now, about—"

"Ramon, I'm going to stop you for a second. Keep that thought for a new poem tucked in the back of your mind. Right now, can we look some more at the poem you started yesterday?" Matter of factly, I said, "You know, poets stay with their poems for a long time to make sure they are exactly how they want them to be, especially if they are poems that the poet really likes. So the fact that you love this poem makes it a good one to work on."

Ramon looked at me with obvious annoyance, like a little racehorse bursting to get out of the stall, but I pressed on. "Ramon, can you read me your poem from yesterday?"

He tucked his head and read aloud. "At Daniel's house, out the window, I saw a boy sprinkling bits of bread for the birds. They ate it."

"You've definitely got a small moment in your poem! I can see the boy, sprinkling bits of bread to the birds. You did a great job showing, not telling, that part."

"Yep," said Ramon, sure of his poetry prowess.

"One thing I'm thinking, though, is that because you have some skill at showing a scene, you probably want to use that skill even more so that readers can see even more of what you saw out the window." I pointed to the bread-sprinkling line and said, "I can imagine the boy sprinkling the bread, which seems like the start of the scene, but I

MID-WORKSHOP TEACHING **Replacing Vague Words with Precise Words: Creating a Class Poetry Wall**

"Writers, can I interrupt you? This classroom is *full* of precise language. Listen to this. Hana was rereading her poem about her dog. 'When my dog wakes up, he goes to the kitchen!' But Hana then circled *goes* and tried other words. Listen: 'When my dog wakes up he *skitters* to the kitchen!'

"Anna was writing a poem about eating ice cream. She could have said that when she eats an ice cream cone it *goes* down her hand, but *goes* wouldn't have shown the *exact* way the ice cream moved down her hand. So she sat there for a little while, really thinking about the exactly right word for how the ice cream traveled down her hand. Finally, she chose the word *dribbles*.

"Writers, because we have so much precise language circulating around our room these days, what do you think about us having a poetry wall? We can hang up bits of poems that show how we're using all of the strategies we're learning. I can get it started by putting up specific lines from the poems I just told you about, but we can also add parts of poems in which you've tried any of the other things on the 'Poetry Decisions that Strengthen Meaning' chart. As you continue writing, if you try something amazing in one of your poems, maybe you'd be willing to copy it onto one of these index cards and put it up here so we can all learn from you."

---

can't see what happened next. Poets go back to the moment, the scene, over and over, asking 'What else happened?' and 'What else can I see?'

"Imagine that moment again. What else did you see out the window? What did the birds do when they got the bread? How many birds were there? Tell me *everything* that you saw out the window! Just like we've talked about how writers of narratives work to show and not tell what's happening, poets do the same—maybe even more."

Ramon closed his eyes for a second. He smiled suddenly and looked at me.

I said, "Okay, Ramon, what did you see? What else can you put into your poem so that you are showing what else happened out the window?"

"Well, it was so funny. When the boy sprinkled the bread, the birds were . . . sort of like they were laughing!" I gestured for him to say more, and he added on. "It was like their heads were just jumping up and down, and then one guy put his head down on his chest, like this." Ramon demonstrated, tucking his small chin down onto his chest, keeping his brown eyes focused on me.

"Ramon, you have *got* to put that into your poem! How will you add your new thinking?"

"I think I can just put it down at the bottom here," he pointed to some empty space at the bottom of his first draft, "about how the birds were laughing."

"Great, Ramon. Get started. Remember that you can do this always. Poets don't just go back to drafts of poems. They also go back to the image, the scene, seeing their subject again, and they ask, 'What else?'"

When I returned close to the end of the workshop, Ramon had added to his writing, and he'd almost finished a draft of a new poem. (See Figure 6–1.)

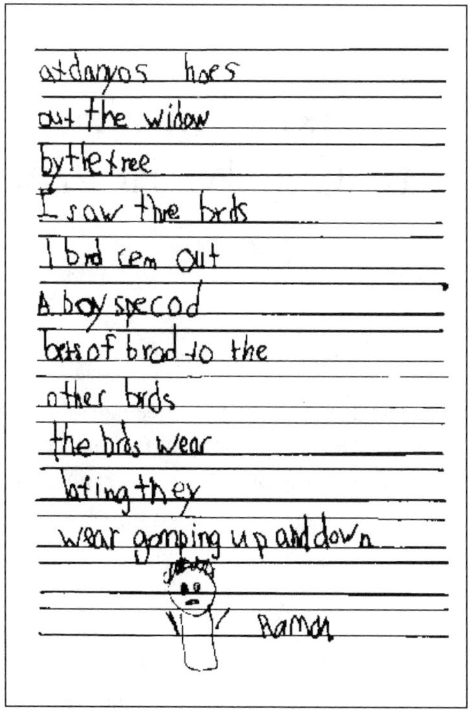

FIG. 6–1 Ramon revisits his subject again, asking "What else?"

At Daniel's House

out the window
by the tree
I saw three birds
one bird came out
A boy sprinkled
bits of bread to the
other birds
the birds were
laughing they
were jumping up and down.

Looking at How Mentor Poets Use Precise Language to Clarify the Image *and* Influence the Sound

Read to children another example of honest, precise language.

"Earlier, at the start of this unit, we read Valerie Worth's poem, "Aquarium." I was reading it again yesterday and I noticed that some of the words seem to be exactly right because of their image *and* their sound. Listen as I read it aloud and notice how the *sounds* of the words match what they are saying about how the fish or the snails move." I read the poem.

> Aquarium
>
> by Valerie Worth
>
> *Goldfish*
> *Flash*
> *Gold and silver scales;*
> *They flick and slip away*
> *Under green weed—*
> *But round brown snails*
> *Stick*
> *To the glass*
> *And stay*

"Did you hear it? The words that go with the goldfish sound the way goldfish move in the water, and the words that describe the snails actually sound . . . snailish. Say, 'flash,' and 'flick.' Now say 'round' and 'brown.'" As I said these words I highlighted the quickness of the short vowels and the sluggishness of the diphthongs. "It feels really different, right?"

Nina started to call out other words in the poem. "Hey, 'slip' is also fast, and 'green weed,' is slow.

"Yeah, I can hear that, too! It would have sounded completely different if she'd written, 'Goldfish shine,' right?"

"Now, listen to this poem by Kristine O'Connell George. We read another one of her poems, 'Between Two Trees,' earlier in the unit. Listen to this one, titled 'Lullaby.' Notice how the words Kristine chose match the feeling of going to sleep."

Lullaby
by Kristine O'Connell George

Tree sighs softly
as the birds patter about
her heavy old branches,
settling down,
tucking their heads
beneath their wings.

She waits until dusk
has shadowed her leaves,
and when she's sure
she's heard that last
soft cheep,

she rocks her birds to sleep.

"I'm noticing words like *softly* and *settling* down. Do you notice any other words?"

"I see soft cheep!" Rowan called out.

"And *she rocks her birds to sleep*." Silas said.

"Great noticing, writers. All of those words give the reader the feeling of going to sleep, don't they? And they also make the poem sound soft and slow. I'm also noticing how the poem slows down toward the end. See the very last line, all by itself, 'she rocks her birds to sleep.'? I think Kristine put that line all by itself because she wants her readers to slow down at the end of the poem to make the sound match the meaning."

Remind children to choose honest, precise words in their own writing.

"Let's really make a commitment to find the best, most specific words for our poems from now on."

Patterning through Repetition

IN THIS SESSION, you'll teach students that poets repeat words, lines, sounds, and images to give their poems rhythm, sound, and music and to bring out the meaning.

GETTING READY

✔ "Go Wind" by Lilian Moore, enlarged on chart paper (see Teaching)

✔ "Poetry Decisions that Strengthen Meaning" chart to add to during the Link

TODAY YOU WILL HELP THE CLASS LEARN about the way poets use the sounds of words, especially repeated patterns, to create effects in poems.

Poets use repetition in many ways. Rather than isolate each way and teach them one by one, you will focus instead on the idea of repetition in general, allowing children freedom to use repetition as they choose. Your students may notice and experiment with circle poems that end as they began. One child may choose to begin each line with the same word or phrase, as Lee Bennett Hopkins does in "Why Poetry?" Other children will repeat especially significant words or lines as a way of highlighting their meaning or adding rhythm. Some may take a lesson from Valerie Worth and use alliteration, repeating initial sounds.

In this session, you will read aloud examples of repetition of words, lines, sounds, and also of images. You will point out that repetition creates patterns of sound. And while it will be natural for your students to notice rhyme, you will not focus on writing rhyming poetry but instead on simpler, more natural uses of repetition for seven- and eight-year-old poets.

After children have heard these patterns, they'll have a chance to read one or two poems aloud together, so they can also internalize the feeling of sound patterns in their own mouths. In his book *Making Your Own Days: The Pleasures of Reading and Writing Poetry*, Kenneth Koch writes, "The musical elements, the sounds that words have, are usually hidden, or mostly hidden. They can be brought out and made hearable by repetition." In this lesson, you will help your young writers bring out the hidden sounds of words in their own poems.

Patterning through Repetition

CONNECTION

Show the children a pattern from the classroom. Remind them that patterns are important in the world.

"This morning, Sarah showed me a necklace she made. Sarah, stand up so everyone can see it. Isn't it beautiful? She made a pattern, didn't she? Can you see the pattern? Note in your mind how the pattern goes on Sarah's necklace." I paused.

"Patterns are really important in the world: we've learned about patterns in math and in art. There are patterns in buildings. If you look at our school from the outside, you see window, window, window, then a big stretch of the wall, then window, window, window, wall. That's a pattern. And Sarah's necklace has five blue beads, then three silver dots, then five blue beads, then three silver dots. That's a pattern. There are patterns all over the place!"

Explain that poets use patterns, too, and that repetition is an important kind of pattern in poetry.

"The reason I'm telling you about Sarah's necklace is that poets think a lot about patterns when they write. Patterns give a poem music!"

❧ **Name the teaching point.**

"Today I want to teach you that poets repeat things—words, sounds, and lines—to give their poems music and to make the meaning of their poems more clear."

One powerful method for teaching a concept is to reduce that concept to its simplest form, teach it in that form, and then show how it translates into more complex situations. Notice that when I make my little speech about patterns, I do so in a way that employs a pattern, an order. It's often wise to make our form match our message.

TEACHING

Show an example of a poem with repetition. Point out one or two patterns, and show children how the poem might sound without them.

"When I read another poet's work I sometimes give myself a specific way to read it. I might say, 'I want to read this and think about how the poet uses patterns and repetition.' Let's look at Lilian Moore's 'Go Wind' and think about repetition."

Go Wind
by Lilian Moore

Go wind, blow
Push wind, swoosh
Shake things
Take things
Make things
fly.

Ring things.
Swing things
Fling things
high.

Go wind, blow
Push things
Wheee.
No, wind, no
Not me—
not me.

"Lilian Moore decided to use lots of repetition. She used repetition for a reason. Let's think *why* she used repetition. How does repetition help her show the meaning of her poem? Hmm." I reread and thought, giving children time to do the same.

"I notice the word *things* is repeated over and over. When I read the lines 'Shake things, Take things, Make things, fly' and 'Ring things, Swing things, Fling things, high,' it feels like the wind is actually rocking me back and forth." I swayed my body from side to side for effect. "Let me read those lines again. See if you can feel the wind. See if the words push you back and forth." I reread and enacted.

"But how exactly did the poet do this? Let's go back and look closely at those lines. 'Shake things, Take things, Make things, fly.' 'Ring things, Swing things, Fling things, high.' Not only did Lilian repeat the word *things*, but she also repeated sounds. Sh*ake* things, T*ake* things, M*ake* things.

"If those repeating patterns weren't there, the music of the poem would sound different. If I said, 'wiggle things, take stuff, push objects around,' instead of 'shake things, take things, make things,' the music would be completely different." I reread the poem, leaving out as much repetition as I could.

Go wind, blow
Push wind, swoosh
Wiggle things
Take stuff
Push objects
around.

Circle some stuff
Swing things
Throw something
up into the air.

No wind, don't
Not me—
Don't blow me away.

ACTIVE ENGAGEMENT

Enlist students to find other patterns in the poem and to notice how repetition enhances the meaning of it.

"What are you noticing, poets? Do you see repetition? Why did the poet make the decisions she did?" I asked, and channeled children to talk. A few minutes later, I said, "Many of you noticed the first two lines are repeated at the start of the third stanza," and I pointed. "Turn and talk for a minute about why Lilian might have done that."

Daniel said, "It's like the wind is coming back again."

Nina answered, "And *high* and *fly* sound kind of windy, but *whee* and *me* sound even more windy! It's getting windier! Maybe she thought those words would sound . . . windy."

"We can't really know what Lilian was thinking, but she probably wrote her poem one way and then another and thought of words, lines, sounds, or images that could be repeated to pop out the music and meaning of her poem. She might have thought, 'How can I use repetition to show that the wind keeps coming back and keeps pushing things around? She could've thought, 'If I write 'ring things, swing things,' those words almost rock you back and forth!' I bet she even asked herself, 'Would repetition give this poem music? Would it match my meaning?'"

I try to find a pattern that is not totally obvious, leaving the more obvious ones for kids to find. As soon as I can, I pass the baton to the kids and ask them to search for patterns, and I want to set them up for success.

Notice that you are using the domain-specific vocabulary that poets use.

Whenever you use published texts as examples, it falls on you to imagine the process the writer probably used to create that text. It does no great harm to say, "Lilian probably thought . . . and she (probably) picked up her pen and then she probably . . ." Yes, you are imagining this, but after all, you do say that word—probably— that signals to children that this is a guess, not a fact.

LINK

Explain to children how today's teaching fits into the larger context of working with music, image, and meaning.

"Let's add one more strategy to our "Poetry Decisions" chart. You saw that repetition of sounds, words, or entire lines not only makes the poem *sound* different but also makes the poem *mean* something different."

Poetry Decisions that Strengthen Meaning

Make Meaning with Images
- Use honest, precise words.
- Show, not tell.

Make Meaning with Music
- Pay attention to line breaks.
- Use patterns and repetition of sounds, words, and lines.

"Today, you may want to go back to a poem that you have already written, to see if there are some revisions that you can make using patterns and repetition. Or you may start off with a fresh idea and a new poem. Keep in mind *all* of the decisions that you can make to strengthen your poem's meaning. So go ahead now and get started!"

Small Groups Support Students' Experimentation with Repetition

IF YOU HAVE A CHANCE TO LOOK OVER YOUR STUDENTS' WORK before the workshop, you can prepare somewhat for your conferring and small-group work. You may want to jot small lists of the children who seem ready for help on one thing, another, and another, so that you'll be able to assemble some small-group instruction.

First and foremost, you'll note children who seem to whip off poems without a lot of effort, writing "any ol' thing." Your expectation is that these youngsters will embrace repetition and repeat in a fairly willy-nilly fashion. You'll want to let them know that thinking about *why* a poet uses repetition is as important as thinking about *how* a

MID-WORKSHOP TEACHING   Exploring Sounds and Meaning

"Eyes up here for a minute, poets. I know you all are working to put exactly what you mean in your poems. At some point today, you might want to take some time to read your poems aloud—the one you are writing today, but also poems that you have already written. As you read the poem aloud to yourself, listen for the sounds that you have included, the sounds that repeat, especially, and think, 'Do these sounds match what I am trying to say? Have I used words that *sound* like the thing I am describing? If you have, poets call that *onomatopoeia.*" I wrote the word on the board and the poets all tried to say it. "To practice, I'll read this poem that Tess has written. It's about icicles when it is warm and sunny and icicles when it is biting cold. Think, first, what sounds you might expect Tess to repeat when it is sssssunny? And what about when it is c-c-c-cold? Listen up, and be ready to talk about whether her poem has onomatopoeia." (See Figure 7–1.)

"Turn and talk, what did you notice?"

The children talked, and many of them noticed that the second portion repeated the /k/ sound, making the poem sound cold and crackly, just like an icicle. In contrast, when the icicle is melting, Tess uses "drip, drip, drop" to describe the melting icicles—onomatopoeia. Then I sent them back to work.

```
                    Icicles
                          by: Tess


Icicles sparkle
in the sun
Drip, drip, drop
Water dropping down
Icicles fade
When the sun comes up
Icicles come to life
When it is cold
Icicles dance in the sky
```

Icicles
by Tess

Icicles sparkle
in the sun
Drip, drip, drop
Water dropping down
Icicles fade
when the sun comes up
Icicles come to life
when it is cold
Icicles dance in the sky

FIG. 7–1   Tess's poem uses onomatopoeia

poet uses repetition. Show children how they can "try on" what the effect would be of repeating different words, sounds, images or phrases in a poem by rereading the poem orally and repeating different parts. As they listen to each oral rendition, they can think aloud about whether that repetition supports what they want to say. To help these youngsters take repetition—and in fact, any craft move—more seriously, you could remind them of the author study they conducted earlier in the year: "Remember how Angela Johnson kept repeating the phrase 'the leaving morning,' to make sure her readers understood just how important that big idea was? What do you think is the most important part of your poem?" You could also channel children to reread familiar poems, asking, "Why might the poet have repeated this part?" Your group members will soon be searching for the key lines or phrases in their poems and exploring ways to use repetition to highlight those parts of their poems. If you are able to do so, use repetition as a way to address the broader issue that sometimes it seems as if the children are whipping out little poems, not taking seriously the challenge to say exactly what they want to say.

Be mindful that just because your minilesson focused on repetition, this does not mean that your conferring and small groups will have the same focus. Instead, your teaching needs to be responsive, addressing whatever your assessments show students most need. It may be, for example, that you decide to issue a new challenge to some of your youngsters. These may be children who are doing a great job writing poetry and who seem ready for a push. You might gather them together and tell them that you studied their work and feel that they are ready for a challenge, and then you could proceed to tell them that many poets have a topic that they return to often, writing a collection of texts about that one topic. Pulitzer Prize–winning writer Don Murray once said to my colleagues and me, "Most writers have just three topics that they return to over and over. Write down your three topics." When Murray said that to us, I was startled—but

quickly found that he was right. It's been almost thirty years since he said that to my colleagues and me, but I recall it often. Try saying something similar to your children. Suggest they might benefit from taking a single topic and writing about that one topic repeatedly, in somewhat different but overlapping ways. When children do this, they are actually engaging in a kind of revision. They'll unearth details, insights, and ideas as they linger with a single topic.

Of course, some of your time will be spent conferring. As you do this, remember to begin your conferences not by studying the student work, but by listening to the writer. "What have you been working on as a poet?" you will probably say. "What have you been trying to do?" When the poet answers, be sure to say, "Can you show me that work?" Expect to look across many poems that the writer has made. If this is a poet who is trying to lay her words out on the page in ways that match her meaning, you'll want to see how she has done that across time, not just in the most recent poem. As you confer, be sure you ask writers the sorts of questions that help them become more analytic as readers of their poetry. "Of all your poems, which do you think does this work the best? Why is this the best?" You might also ask, "How would this have had a different effect if you had . . . " After researching for longer than is your tendency, think to yourself, "What are the most important things I could teach this writer?" Your knowledge of the topic will help you to not feel empty-handed. For example, the fact that you already know that the key to craft decisions is that they must highlight meaning means that if the writer is working on a poem about feeling lonely, you have the option to teach the writer that she may want to isolate the line in which she stands alone at the window, or to highlight forlorn vowel sounds. But you need to be ready to teach something entirely different because of what you learn during the research component of the conference.

Reading Aloud to Find Places for Revision

Provide an opportunity for poets to say their poems out loud to each other, using reading aloud as a way to listen for opportunities for revision.

"Partner 1, when I say go, read the poem you've been working on out loud to Partner 2. As you read, make your voice emphasize the part that repeats so that both you and Partner 2 can hear how it sounds. Partner 2, as you listen, remember to pay attention not only to how the repetition sounds, but also to whether it brings out the poem's meaning. If it's not quite working, let your partner know. He or she might try it in a different spot or repeat something else altogether. In a couple minutes, you two will switch roles. Go!"

The room filled with the sound of children's poems. I circled the room and listened in. Ainsley was reading to Reed, pausing dramatically after each time she said "Just my mom." (See Figure 7–2.)

"Poets," I said, calling the class together. "Did you see how reading aloud really helps you pay attention to the way your poems sound? Whenever you're writing—not just poems but other kinds of writing as well—it can help to read your text aloud, both to yourself and to someone else. That way, you can hear if it is working or if you need to go back and revise."

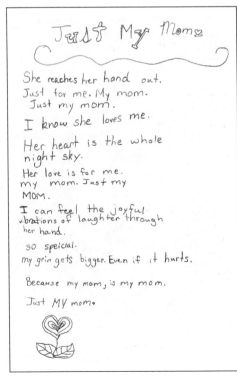

FIG. 7–2 Ainsley pauses dramatically at "Just my mom" during read-aloud

Just My Mom
by Ainsley

She reaches her hand out.
Just for me. My mom.
Just my mom.
I know she loves me.
Her heart is the whole
night sky.
Her love is for me.
My mom. Just my
MOM.
I can feel the joyful
vibrations of laughter through
her hand.
So special.
My grin gets bigger. Even if it hurts.
Because my mom, is my mom.
Just MY mom.

Poems Are Moody

IN THIS SESSION, you'll teach students that poets consider the mood they want to convey, and they make sure that the mood matches the poem's meaning.

GETTING READY

✔ Student poem that captures a clear mood, written on chart paper (see Connection)

✔ "Way Down in the Music" by Eloise Greenfield, enlarged on chart paper (see Teaching)

✔ "Poem" by Langston Hughes, enlarged on chart paper (see Teaching)

✔ "Poetry Decisions that Strengthen Meaning" chart to add to during the Link

A S YOUNG PEOPLE BECOME MORE SKILLED and knowledgeable as writers, one of the big steps that you will see them take is that they will begin to think less about their content and more about their craft. This is not an easy step to take. Even fifth graders tend to gravitate toward strategies for generating ideas more than toward strategies for making their language powerful, their images memorable. This session is one of many in this unit that places an emphasis squarely on craft. There is almost no talk at all about youngsters needing to think about what they will write. The emphasis, instead, is on how they will write. More specifically, the emphasis is on poets needing to choose the tone, the mood, their voice.

World-class standards make a very big deal of children learning to read analytically, noticing how an author goes about writing a topic. Upper-grade students are asked to be able to compare-and-contrast how two different authors wrote on the same topic. The good news is that this session starts children on the journey toward being able to talk about an author's choices. In the minilesson, you contrast ways in which you could have written about a topic, and try to help youngsters know that your language choices need to match your meaning.

You'll set children up to write-in-the-air the way they would describe waking up in the morning if their message and mood was one thing, and if it was quite the opposite.

Through all this work, you are expanding the palette that youngsters draw on in order to write. You are helping them develop an increasing sense of authorial intention, or artistic power. The lessons are important ones not only for your children as writers but also for them as readers.

Poems are Moody

CONNECTION

Point out that the weather has moods, and so, too, do poems.

"Writers, have you ever noticed that when you write, you choose not only words, but also the weather? And the weather can be moody. Right now, think about this: when the mood is cheery, carefree, happy as a lark, what will the matching weather be?" I gave them a few seconds to think. "Now think, when the mood is brooding, sullen, with bottled up anger, what will the weather be?

"Poems, also, have moods, and those moods come from all the decisions that a poet has made."

Share an example of a poem that has a voice—for example, of awe or respect—and point out how the poet's decisions reflect that voice.

"I'm going to read a poem to you, and will you think about how you could describe the mood of this poem? This is by Rowan." (See Figure 8–1.)

"Turn and talk. What's the mood you hear in this poem?" As children talked, I coached them to reach for precise, specific words that exactly conveyed what they wanted to say.

◆ COACHING

It is a big deal for a writer to learn that he or she can make the weather in a text match the mood that he or she wants to convey.

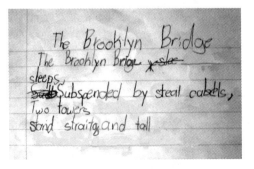

The Brooklyn Bridge
The Brooklyn Bridge
sleeps,
Suspended by steel cables,
Two towers
stand straight and tall

FIG. 8–1 Rowan's poem inspires awe.

Many children said the mood was one of respect—awe even. I repeated this to the class. "Rowan knew he wanted the poem to have that mood, so he used words that would be awe-inspiring—strong steel cables and straight, tall towers. He didn't show the cars rattling over the bridge, the honking of the horns, and the bicycler weaving in and out of the traffic. That information wouldn't go into a poem that was meant to show the awe Rowan feels for the bridge.

"It's not just the details he chose to include and those he chose not to include that helped his poem convey a mood of awe. It's also the sound of the poem. Let me read it again, and see if you can hear that this poem *sounds* a bit like the bridge looks." I reread the poem.

❖ **Name the teaching point.**

"Today I want to teach you that poets consider the mood they want their poems to convey. They write, thinking about the mood, and they reread their poems and ask, 'Does the mood match the meaning?'"

TEACHING

Read aloud several poems with contrasting moods. Liken the poems to songs, suggesting there are different kinds of songs.

"Just to get you used to thinking about the moods in poetry, will you listen with me to these two poems? Pay attention to the mood of each poem. I think you'll notice that they have very different moods. I then read "Way Down in the Music," by Eloise Greenfield, and "Poem," by Langston Hughes. I read them in such a way as to highlight, but not exaggerate, the differences in mood.

When you want to make a point, one of the best ways to do so is through contrasting examples. There are some other things to notice here. First, you set children up beforehand so they know what they are listening for. Then too, you are returning to familiar texts. All of these are moves that you'll see time and again in minilessons.

> Way Down in the Music
>> by Eloise Greenfield
>
> *I get way down in the music*
> *Down inside the music*
> *I let it wake me*
> *Take me*
> *Spin me around and make me*
> *Uh-get down.*

> Poem
>> by Langston Hughes
>
> *I loved my friend.*
> *He went away from me.*
> *There's nothing more to say.*
> *The poem ends,*
> *Soft as it began—*
> *I loved my friend.*

70

"Earlier we said that a poem is like the song that a poet's heart is singing. Well, those songs might be dancing songs or losing-a-friend songs, funny songs or mad songs . . . " As I let my voice trail off, a couple of children picked up the thread.

"They could be new-baby-sister songs," said Maddie.

"Or mad-at-my-friend songs," said Nina.

"And the important thing is that when poets write, they want the sounds of the poems to combine with the words and with the details to create a mood. When Langston Hughes wrote his poem about losing a friend, he wanted the sound and the meaning to combine to make the poem *sound* sad and also *say* sad things. It would have been crazy if his poem about his friend moving away had sounded like this," and with a bouncy rhythm, I chanted happily:

> *Hey, you guys,*
> *Guess what's new?*
> *My friend's moving away*
> *Watcha gonna do?*

The kids chuckled a little at how silly this sounded. "That doesn't make sense, right? That would be a made-a-new-friend voice, not a losing-my-friend voice. Let's see, if Langston Hughes had wanted to make his poem angry instead of sad, what might he have done? I'm thinking about what I do, what I sound like, when I'm mad." I paused.

> *How dare he!*
> *Move away?*
> *The nerve.*
> *I could slam the door in his face.*

"Let me stop. Do you see how I used short stabbing lines when I was trying to make an angry version of Hughes's poem? I'd want to reread it and think, 'Does this *really* sound mad?' and to try it again and again. My point is that in his poem, Langston made all kinds of decisions that go with the losing-my-friend message he wanted to convey."

ACTIVE ENGAGEMENT

Invite kids to try saying a poem in different moods, using images and music that reflect the mood. Give them the topic, the content, and let them work on the mood.

"Now it's your turn to try it. Pretend you are writing about waking up in your bed. You are just about to wake up, and you feel the warm sun. Partner 1, tell Partner 2 a poem with a loving voice. Picture it. What is an image that goes with loving the sun? How will the sound of this poem match the mood? You are lying in bed, just starting to wake up. You feel the warm sun on you, and . . . what? Turn and make up a quick poem with your partner." The children began reciting sweet poems about the sun.

Be sure that your intonation highlights your point. Minilessons are not a time for subtlety. Be over-the-top. Get kids to laugh a bit. A minilesson works if it is memorable, and the way you deliver the minilesson plays a big role in that.

I sequence my comments so the last thing I say sets up the children for just what I want them to do. This provides a lot of support.

"Writers, I heard such loving poems," I said. "Anna said, 'Sun, warming my face, telling me it's a new day.' Anna decided that the image of the sun warming her face really goes with a loving voice.

"Now let's imagine it with an angry mood. Picture it. Think about the image *and* the sound, or music! Ready? Turn and tell each other your poems."

I heard Sarah say, "Too bright! Too bright! Can't you see I'm sleeping in here?"

Daniel added, "Listen, you hot ball of gas! You're shining right in my eye!"

"The poems you are making now have a very different mood than the loving-the-sun poem. Poems, like the weather, can be moody."

LINK

Remind poets that they have learned about many kinds of poetry decisions and that they can also make decisions to reflect the voice—or mood—they are trying to convey.

"When you get to work today, if you are starting a new poem, you might want to decide what the mood of your poem will be, and pause as you draft and reread, thinking, 'Does this match the mood I want?' We'll add the fact that poets think about mood onto this new part of our chart, Poetry Decisions that Strengthen Meaning.

"Remember to read your poem aloud as you go. If anyone wants more help with giving a poem voice, stay behind on the carpet and I'll help you. The rest of you—off you go."

Share one example of this kind of mood—but one example is enough. You have several other moods to illustrate.

The easiest kind of active engagement would be to say, "Turn to your partner and say back three ways to create a different mood through the voice of your poem." That'd be a fine option, but it's always preferable to get children to do what you want them to do rather than talk about it.

Poetry Decisions that Strengthen Meaning

Make Meaning with Images
- Use honest, precise words.
- Show, not tell.

Make Meaning with Music
- Pay attention to line breaks.
- Use patterns and repetition of sounds, words, and lines.

Put It All Together
- Decide on the mood and bring it out.

Capturing Mood in a Poem Is Complicated!

IN OUR EFFORTS TO MAKE COMPLICATED IDEAS FEEL MORE ACCESSIBLE, we sometimes have to offer one way a writer might do something, though we know there are many more ways. This session shows students the power of letting mood guide decisions about voice and suggests that poems have a single mood, such as that of losing a friend or winning a prize. But, of course, a poem can have shifts in mood. When you confer today, you may need to look out for students who are trying with frustration to squeeze their poems into the poems-have-one-mood lesson.

Perhaps you'll pull these students aside and suggest that poets find different ways to give a poem mood. You might then share a couple poems that show clear differentiation from the ones with which you modeled during today's lesson. These don't have to be published poems; you could model with ones you have written for this distinct purpose. One poem might show a shift in mood; maybe at first things feel light and then they get heavy (or vice versa). Another poem might even go back and forth, with the narrator feeling one way (or the poem conveying one tone), then another. A poem about wanting to try something new might convey excitement, then fear, excitement, then fear.

You could also hearken back to earlier teaching that emphasized that poets anchor big feelings in small objects or images to suggest that moods, too, can be anchored in objects and images. A poem with a heavy mood might include a physically heavy object, such as a boulder, or a thunder cloud, or an image of something broken, as in Jasper's poem about a skull he sketched from the nature table. (See Figure 8–2.)

(continues)

MID-WORKSHOP TEACHING   Kids Invent Their Own Tools to Help Them Capture Mood in Their Poems

"Writers, some of you are going back over all your old poems and thinking about whether the mood in those poems matches the meaning you want to convey. That's a smart decision. Watching you do this work, there are a couple of really cool inventions that you all have made. I want Wyatt to show you one of these."

Wyatt stood up. "When I read my poems to myself, if I really want to hear them, I make my hand into a seashell," he said, and demonstrated that he has found that if he fists his hand into a conch shell shape and reads into his hand—actually voicing the poem into his hand—while he meanwhile cups one of his ears, he can really listen to the draft of his poem. "Then I can choose how it goes," he announced.

While the class took a turn trying Wyatt's invention, Josie stood up and, after I helped her retrieve the kids' attention, she showed the class that she'd found that some of her poems needed to have two moods—like maybe a mad mood at the start and then a happy mood at the end. As she wrote, she made little faces (smiley or otherwise) in the margins to remind her of the mood she wanted to show.

"I'm sure many of you are coming up with your own ways to make your poems have moods and to make them show the meanings you want to convey. Remember as you write that poets go to the ends of the earth to accomplish their goals. Keep writing. You have twenty more minutes of writing time."

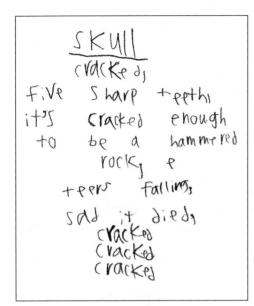

FIG. 8–2 Jasper anchors the image of something broken into his poem.

Skull

by Jasper

cracked,
Five sharp teeth,
it's cracked enough
to be a hammered
rock,
tears falling
sad it died,
cracked
cracked
cracked

A poem with a lighter mood, on the other hand, might feature a feather or a leaf. Children in the group could work together to come up with other representational images; they could use their senses to think about how something looks or tastes or feels to the touch might also convey a mood. Here, of course, you'll likely have an opportunity to introduce the fact that poets see things differently not only from other people, but from one another. One kid's idea of a delicious, happy smell (onions cooking in butter) may be another kid's idea of torture. These are important ideas to bring into a conversation about mood in poems.

Using Point of View to Express Poetic Voice

Share a voice that a child has discovered.

As students gathered together on the rug, I asked Nathan to come up to the front. "Listen to what Nathan wrote. He wrote a poem from the point of view of a book. He has really tried to see things as a book would if it had eyes. Sometimes poets try on other points of view besides their own when they are writing. Here's the thing: if you write a poem from a different point of view, then the voice in the poem needs to sound like that point of view. Okay, Nathan, go ahead and read." (See Figure 8–3.)

Channel the class to consider whether they might write a poem from a different point of view, and set them up to write-in-the-air.

Then I said to the class, "Will you look through your folders of poems and find one that is about something—about your mother, about a bird, about a bridge—that could be rewritten so that the subject does the talking? That would mean that the next draft of the poem might be written as if your mother is talking—or the bird or the bridge. Give me a thumbs up when you have found a poem that could possibly be rewritten so it is in the voice of what is now the topic." I waited until many children had signaled, and then said, "Will you write-in-the-air, speaking in the voice of that subject, and try making an out-loud-poem?" They did, and I reminded children that this was something they might want to do tomorrow.

A Good Book to Read
Turn my pages
full of words!
read information
or a good tale.
I'm stuck on a shelf
Until somebody gets me.
I did get read
I have good pictures.
The boy loves to read me.

by, Nathan

FIG. 8–3   Nathan's poem is from the point of view of a book.

A Good Book to Read
by Nathan

Turn my pages
full of words!
Read information
or a good tale.

I'm stuck on a shelf
Until somebody gets me.

I did get read
I have good pictures.
The boy loves to read me.

Using Comparisons to Clarify Feelings and Ideas

IN THIS SESSION, you'll teach students that one way poets make meaning is to compare one thing to another.

GETTING READY

✓ Chart with two columns, first column titled "Ordinary Language" with a list of ordinary sentences and the second column titled "Comparative Language." The second column will be blank so you can add to it during the teaching.

✓ "Poetry Decisions that Strengthen Meaning" chart, to add to during the Link.

✓ "Inside My Heart" by Zoë Ryder White, written on chart paper (see Mid-Workshop Teaching)

I F YOU ASK J. PATRICK LEWIS, Children's Poet Laureate of the United States (2011–2013), about the power of metaphor, he may respond with a poem. Each stanza of "Everything Is a Poem," in the forthcoming *Everything Is a Poem: The Selected Best of J. Patrick Lewis*, compares a poem to a concrete image in the world. The poem concludes with:

> A busy bee's a poem
> With nectar that's so fine
> A reader-eater laps up every
> Honey of a line.
>
> This winding path's a poem
> Meandering through the woods
> Of real or imaginary
> Eerie neighborhoods
> That poets like to navigate
> In search of either/or—
> One thing can mean another: that's
> What metaphors are for.

If one of your goals in this unit is to help children relish and play with language, then you'll need to take the plunge into the deep water of figurative language. Although it is true that poets seek out honest, precise words, this is true of all writers. Poets, more than other writers, use metaphor, simile, and personification to convey their meaning. World-class standards expect second-graders to demonstrate understanding of figurative language, word relationships, and nuances in word meanings. This session and the one that follows specifically engage children in exploring and using figurative language with intention and purpose.

You may worry that these techniques are out of your children's reach, but the truth is that seven-year-olds have a special kinship with metaphor. The young child sees a leaf spin to the ground and says, "It's flying!" She notices an acorn with its shell still on and decides it is a magic elf. A wagon is an airplane, a line of chairs is a train, a pile of pots is a collection of kettledrums. They use simile and metaphor naturally and without self-consciousness. "He had a jelly bean bald head," a youngster said to me. "This towel is my Rapunzel hair." "My pancake is swimming in an ocean of syrup." It's wise to nudge children to use figurative language, and now is a good time to introduce them to the domain-specific terms as well. The children will be eager to learn this domain-specific vocabulary, and although they may not always use terms such as *alliteration* and *metaphor* correctly, they'll be chomping at the bit to know and use the vocabulary that professionals use. Make the most of this. Let children know that whereas one way to convey big feelings is by showing, not telling, another way is by comparing the feelings to something else.

Many people will tell you that the best time to learn a new

"Poets, more than other writers, use metaphor, simile, and personification to convey their meaning."

language is when you are very young, and this is as true for poetic language as for Spanish or Arabic. The advantage of learning a new language when you are young is that people welcome approximating. You've recently encouraged your children to take on the language of poetry. They will have only just begun to use metaphor and simile consciously and will need lots more time for approximation. Earlier you made a great point of appreciating their invented spellings. "Just spell it as best you can," you said to them. Now you'll want to be equally supportive of their invented simile and metaphor. "Just describe things the best you can," you'll say.

Using Comparisons to Clarify Feelings and Ideas

CONNECTION

Tell students that one way poets see with poets' eyes is to compare things, ideas, or feelings to something else.

"Poets, we've talked a lot about how poems have big feelings but are also about small objects that hold big feeling. We started this unit by seeing objects with poets' eyes. Poets see the whole world, inside and out of themselves, with poets' eyes. Do you remember when we studied how Zoë saw the ceiling in a fresh way—as a sky—and she imagined the pencil sharpener had bees buzzing around inside it? And remember when we all tried to see our pine cones and our feathers with fresh eyes, comparing them to other things? Well, do you know what? Poets are always comparing things to other things. Poets even compare their big feelings to things they picture, to images."

Name the teaching point.

"Today I want to teach you that one way poets make meaning in their poems is to compare an object or a feeling—or anything at all—to something else."

TEACHING

Show children how to revise ordinary phrases to include comparisons (comparative language), by picturing what the ordinary phrase seems like or reminds you of.

"When I'm writing a poem, I try to make my meaning even stronger by turning ordinary lines into lines where I use comparisons. That is called 'using comparative language.' I think about ways that my feeling or my topic reminds me of something else in the world, and then I write what that thing is. Let's look at some ordinary language, and then I'll show you how I say the same thing in a more meaningful way by using a comparison."

I unveiled a chart with two columns. In the first column, labeled "Ordinary Language," I had written several sentences. The second column, labeled "Comparative Language," was empty. "These sentences are ordinary. I say what I see or do in a regular way, not in a poetic way. I'm going to go through and revise these to include a comparison. Will you

Remember to use the exact same phrases you used earlier. If you try to say the same thing in different ways, some children won't comprehend that you are simply reiterating something you said earlier.

Annie Dillard once said of her writing, "I have all my Christmas tree ornaments but no Christmas tree." This has lingered with me. It is easy to use minilessons as a method for dumping doodads on kids. The problem is that no one can remember a hundred unrelated points. We can, however, remember particular bits of advice if they hang together. It's wise, then, to try to provide the Christmas tree as well as the ornaments in your minilessons. In today's lesson, you try to suggest that children have been learning lots of ways to see with poets' eyes—that's what holds this lesson together with others— and comparisons are just one new way to do so.

help me picture what the sentence is saying and then ask, 'What can we compare this to?' Then we'll write a new sentence—one that makes a comparison."

Ordinary Language	Comparative Language
The children kept jumping up to say more ideas.	
My heart was happy.	
When I get to school early, the classroom is quiet.	
The sky is blue.	
He felt sad.	
The clouds are puffy and white.	
She was really shy.	
We line up like a train.	

"Okay, 'The children kept jumping up to say more ideas.' I bet you can picture all of you guys doing that, because you are always so full of ideas! Do you have a picture of this in your mind?" Students nodded, and I continued, "What does this remind me of? What can we compare it to? Hmm." By now, children were on their knees, ready with input, but I guessed that for just this one time, I could demonstrate.

"Well, sometimes when you're very excited about something, you're kind of popping up all over the rug. It reminds me of popcorn!"

Debrief, unpacking the work you have just done.

"Do you see how picturing it helped me think of a comparison? Now I'll write a new sentence on this side of the chart." I pointed to the "Comparative Language" side of the chart.

I spoke as I wrote the revised sentence. "'Ideas popcorned around the classroom.' Do you see how ordinary language says what actually happened, and comparative language shows what the event, the time, or the thing was like? When one of you and then another of you jump up with ideas, I can say, 'Ideas are popcorning around the room,' but your ideas aren't really popcorn. Isn't that a poetic image?"

You'll see throughout this series that when I want to highlight a feature of writing, I often show the same bit of writing without the feature and then with it. This only works if the before and after versions are kept absolutely similar except for the one feature I'm hoping to spotlight. That is, if I want to say that descriptions are more effective if they include sensory details and my before version shows me sitting on my front stoop watching people walk along the sidewalk, my next version can't be of me sitting in the park. If only two old people walk along the sidewalk in my before version, the same two people—and only them—need to be there in the after version.

ACTIVE ENGAGEMENT

Ask the children, with their partners, to revise the remaining ordinary phrases to include comparative language. Collect their ideas and use them to complete the chart.

"Let's try some of these together. Can you and your partner work on one or more of the remaining ordinary sentences? Remember to picture the content of the sentence and ask yourself, 'What does this seem like? What does this remind me of? Choose whichever one you would like to get started with."

Partners quickly got to work as I got down onto the rug to listen in. As expected, I heard a range of responses. Some students stayed very close to the literal ("The clouds remind me of fluffy clouds in the sky."), while others nearly lost sight of the literal on their flights of fancy ("The line reminds me of a big snake that goes down a hole to chase a mouse."). I took note of these approximations, planning a possible small-group lesson. I collected a few ideas and called the class back together to share them.

"Poets! You thought of such interesting comparative language! Here are a few examples that I overheard."

> The clouds are like cotton balls in the sky.
> He felt as sad as the last piece of candy.
> We line up like a train.
> When I get to school, the classroom is sleeping.

"Wow, just look at all these exciting ways we have found to say what happened and how we felt. Comparing things is such a powerful tool in poetry. We just did this with some sentences I wrote on a chart, but soon you'll have a chance to try this in your own poems. Remember that when poets make a decision to do something like repeat words or compare things, they do it to make an image clearer, add music, *and* match their meaning."

LINK

Remind the children that whenever they write, they can use comparisons to help readers get a clear image of what it is they are writing about.

"Whenever you write—and especially whenever you write poetry—if you want readers to really feel and see and hear what you are saying, one thing you can do is to use comparisons. I'm going to add this to our growing chart of 'Poetry Decisions that Strengthen Meaning.' If you want to try this and feel like you need extra help, stay on the rug. The rest of you, get started."

This active engagement gives children lots of repeated practice saying things poetically. Be sure to let children work with partners so that every child has a chance to do this as best he or she can. If you bypass this phase and instantly begin to elicit suggestions from the whole group, a large percentage of the class will just sit back and let others do the work (and get the practice).

Obviously you could list many more possibilities, but you'll quickly make your point. It's time for children to write.

This is a common and very effective way to make your instruction multilevel. Some teachers frequently say, "If you need extra help, stay on the rug. The rest of you, get started."

Poetry Decisions that Strengthen Meaning

Make Meaning with Images

- Use honest, precise words.
- Show, not tell.

Make Meaning with Music

- Pay attention to line breaks.
- Use patterns and repetition of sounds, words, and lines.

Put It All Together

- Decide on the mood and bring it out.
- Compare a feeling or object—or anything at all—to something else.

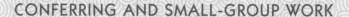

Using Small Groups to Support Students with Comparative Language and Spelling

YOU INVITED STUDENTS who wanted some help making metaphors to stay in the meeting area—on the carpet. You might as well start with suggesting they look together at the carpet. "So let me show you what I mean about how poets compare. I'm just looking at this blue carpet, and I'm thinking, I could compare it to . . . a sea! Our carpet is like the sea, and we're what? Could we say that we're an island of friends? Or . . . " Trail off and allow students to discuss other metaphors to use to describe the small group gathered on the sea of carpet. Then perhaps you will press on, giving them an opportunity to practice again.

"You can do the same with your pencil. So, watch me write and think, 'What can we compare the pencil to?' When I write, it's like my pencil is . . . What?" I gave students time to think then jotted some of their suggestions.

"Remember that poets compare their feelings to other things too. Think of a time you felt peaceful. What was that like?" I again left a pool of silence. "Like a kite on a spring day, Silas? What a beautiful comparison!"

Try to be ready to go with whatever children invent. You'll want to support their approximations, knowing they'll grow into this over time. After a bit of small-group practice, you might ask the children to get out whatever poems they worked on yesterday. Then you could quickly scan the pile and find one that seems promising. Look for a poem that addresses a subject many of the kids know. Then ask all of the group members to help the writer of that one poem imagine how he could bring some "comparing" into his poem. After this metaphor support, your students will be ready to play with some lines of their own poems.

Of course, you won't want all your conferring and small-group work to be channeled toward children who need help getting started. You may also want to convene a small group of youngsters who, with a nudge from you, could sail with the concepts you taught today. Perhaps you'll collect a few children who have especially rich imaginations—those who already turn sticks into wands, lasers, and wizards' canes

---

MID-WORKSHOP TEACHING
Capturing Big Feelings with Figurative Language

"You have all been making lots of comparisons in your poems today, and I'd like you to hear this new poem, 'Inside My Heart,' by Zoë. She wanted to write about how the things that happen in her life matter to her and make her heart full, but she didn't just want to say, 'Oh, my heart is so full! I am so happy!' Listen to how Zoë compares her big feeling to all kinds of things."

Inside My Heart
by Zoë Ryder White

Inside my heart lives
one birthday party
two jazz bands
three wrestling puppies
four dancing birds
five laughing babies
six blasting spaceships
seven lucky fireflies and
a sky full of stars.

"Zoë doesn't just come right out and tell us how she feels. She makes the poem show what she feels by comparing her feelings to things in the world that remind her of that feeling. Dancing birds, laughing babies, and birthday parties are all happy things. By saying in her heart lives those happy things, Zoë shows us that she is happy."

during play time—and you can help those children find mentor poems in books that could help them take their good work to higher levels. You might encourage those children to take lessons from whatever the authors have done. For example, the titles alone merit study. Children are apt to notice, with your help, that many of their poem titles are labels, and they'll discover lots of other options in mentor poems. They'll see that some poems are titled in ways that match their first lines, some give little hints to the deeper meaning. Your goal is that children will realize they can discover new exemplar texts, incorporating what they learn into their own poems.

Although this unit of study is on poetry, you'll want to be sure your conferences and small groups support children's general development as writers. Spend some time focusing on children who need special support with spelling. Notice whether children are spelling long, challenging words in chunks rather than letter by letter. The words they know should automatically give them lots of word power, but you may need to teach children to think, "What words do I know that can help me with *this* word?"

You may notice that a group of your children are misspelling a certain chunk—perhaps an ending—in similar ways. Are many of them spelling the ending *ly* as *le*? If you see a group of children who could profit from similar help, pull them together. Tell them what you have noticed. Ask them to reread, searching for places where they made the error, and to fix those places. (This will give them repeated practice.) Suggest they work together to list words they *might* use that have the spelling pattern.

Using Comparisons to Add or Build Meaning

Read two or three examples of children's poems with fresh comparisons, pointing out ways that the poets used comparisons to build meaning.

"Writers, listen to how Ban compares winter, and all of the seasons, to a person. (See Figure 9–1.)

> Last is
> Winter with cold pink toes.

"And, in her poem, Leela makes her stones do things that are human. Poets call this *personification*. Do you hear the word *person* in there? Leela makes stones into people! Listen." (See Figure 9–2.)

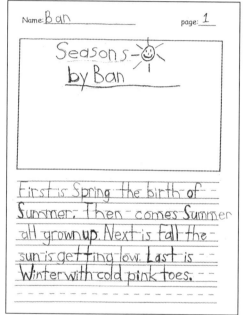

FIG. 9–1   Ban compares seasons to a person.

Stones

by Leela

Bumpy little creatures
Clanking
On each other
Like boys
Fighting

So small
That I wonder
How they weigh
Anything
Little marks
Tell me stories
About their
Adventures
At sea

"And look at how Silas compares tiles to a puzzle, giving his poem an almost sad and lost feeling." (See Figure 9–3.)

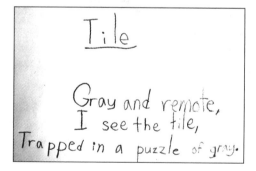

FIG. 9–3   Silas compares a tile to a puzzle.

Tile

Gray and remote,
I see the tile,
Trapped in a puzzle of gray.

FIG. 9–2   Leela personifies stones in her poem.

Stretching Out a Comparison

WHEN PLANNING A UNIT OF STUDY, it's not hard to generate a nice long list of possible topics that fit under the unit umbrella. There are zillions of things that very young children could learn about almost any aspect of writing. In a study of poetry, you can choose to study topic choice, structure, repetition, line breaks, titles, alliteration, metaphor, imagery, personification, and a million other options.

The challenge in planning a writing curriculum is to map out a learning journey that enables children not only to hear about topics but also to approach, experiment with, develop, and extend their skills. Rigor comes not from exploring the surface of a subject, but from deep dives.

After yesterday's lesson, some of your students may be writing poems that list one metaphor after another: the robin outside the window is a dancer, an artist, a construction worker. In today's minilesson, however, you'll teach your class how to stay with, develop, and sustain a single comparison. You'll show children that just as they can take one moment in time and stretch it out across a sequence of pages, so too can they take a comparison and stretch it out across a sequence of lines in a poem. This is another way to use metaphor. If a robin is an artist, it can remain an artist through many lines, as we see in this poem by Amy Ludwig VanDerwater.

Robin
by Amy Ludwig VanDerwater

An artist lives in our old tree.
She works with mud and wood and fur
to build a sturdy twig collage.
Her masterpiece is small like her.
Blue eggs will nestle in this art
framed by branches way up high.
An artist lives in our old tree.
Her museum is the sky.

IN THIS SESSION, you'll teach students that one way poets make a comparison powerful is to stretch it across many lines, adding in actions that go with the comparison.

GETTING READY

- ✔ "Lullaby" by Kristine O'Connell George, enlarged on chart paper (see Teaching)

- ✔ "Comparative Language" chart, made in Session 9 (see Teaching)

- ✔ A poem you have written on chart paper based on one of the items from the "Comparative Language" column; this poem should be in need of revision as it only has one line stating the comparison (see Teaching)

- ✔ A second poem written on chart paper based on another one of the items from the "Comparative Language" column; this poem should also have only one line stating the comparison (See Active Engagement)

- ✔ Chart paper and marker

- ✔ "Poetry Decisions that Strengthen Meaning" chart (see Active Engagement and Share)

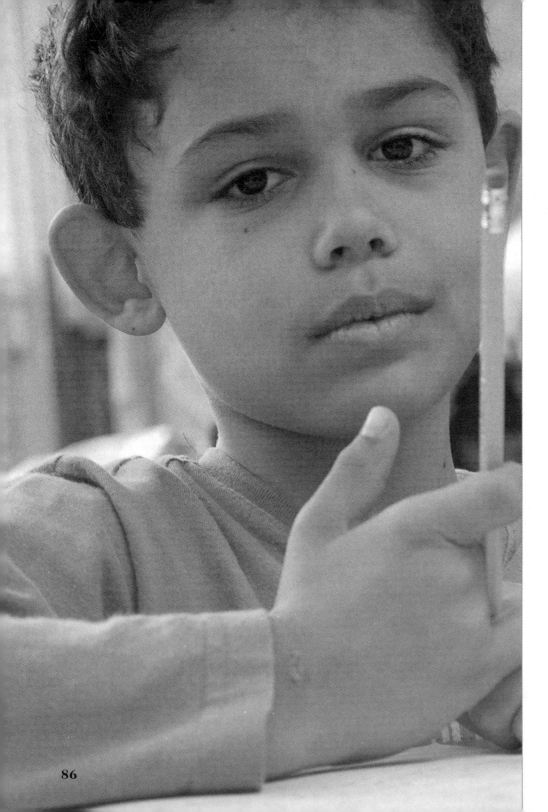

Teaching students to stay with a comparison throughout a poem does not mean that we do not celebrate the myriad of metaphors children will create. It simply means that children will now understand that listing many metaphors serves a different purpose than staying with one comparison through a whole poem. In the same way that talking with many people at a party is different from settling into a long conversation with one friend, writers learn to use metaphors to suit their writing goals.

"Rigor comes not from exploring the surface of a subject, but from deep dives."

Stretching Out a Comparison

CONNECTION

Celebrate students' early work with comparative language, and motivate them to enrich that work.

"You have all done a wonderful job using comparative language in your poems, and the comparisons you have included in your poetry will help your readers get a clear image of the way you feel about your topic. Listen to these great comparisons: Leela wrote that a shell is like armor, and Carolyn wrote that the moon is like a big pearl glowing in the night sky. Turn and tell your neighbor about one comparison you tried yesterday."

After the students finished sharing, I continued, "It's hard to believe, but not long ago, when you were learning how to read, many of you would read for a just few minutes and then you would need a break. These days, you can stay with a book for a very long time. Well, I am thinking that maybe now you are ready to stay with a comparison for a longer time too, stretching your metaphors out over many lines."

❖ Name the teaching point.

"Today I want to teach you that a way to make a comparison even more powerful is to stick with it. A comparison can stretch all the way through a poem. One way to do this is to include actions that go along with the comparison."

TEACHING

Return to the mentor poem "Lullaby" by Kristine O'Connell George and draw students' attention to how she stretches out the comparison across the entire poem.

"Children, I was reading 'Lullaby' by Kristine O'Connell George again and I noticed something. Kristine uses a comparison in her poem—she compares the tree to a person, a mother-like figure. In her poem, the tree lulls the birds to sleep. Listen as I reread this poem."

Highlighting some of the previous wonderful metaphors at the beginning of today's lesson is like a small celebration, an echo leading into today's work. This second day focusing on comparisons in writing will give some students a chance to try this out for the first time, and it will give others an opportunity to build on their work.

SESSION 10: STRETCHING OUT A COMPARISON   **87**

Lullaby
by Kristine O'Connell George

Tree sighs softly
as the birds patter about
her heavy old branches,
settling down,
tucking their heads
beneath their wings.

She waits until dusk
has shadowed her leaves,
and when she's sure
she's heard that last
soft cheep,

she rocks her birds to sleep.

"Do you hear the comparison, writers? She doesn't just compare the tree to a mother one time, or in one line, she stretches that comparison across all her lines. Here," I pointed to the first line in the poem "where she personifies the tree and says 'Tree sighs softly,' all the way to here," I pointed to the last line in the poem, "'she rocks her birds to sleep.' Kristine really sticks with her comparison, doesn't she? And she uses actions—*sighs* and *rocks to sleep*—to really stretch that comparison across her poem."

Refer to the comparative language chart. Show the class a poem you wrote earlier in which the comparison exists in only one line, demonstrating how you can extend it.

"Writers, I bet we could try this out in the poems we write. Let's go back to the chart of comparisons we made yesterday. If I write a poem about this one—'When I get to school early, the classroom is quiet'—I *could* write it like this."

First Version

Mornings
I come in
The classroom is sleeping.
I push chairs in and straighten tables.
Then the children come.

"In my poem, I just quickly *mention* the idea that the classroom is asleep. I only compare the classroom to a sleeping person quickly, in one line. That comparison isn't in the first or second lines," I pointed to those lines. "It *is* in the third

For expediency's sake, I had this version already written. I'd written a very brief poem that doesn't illustrate a host of extraneous aspects of poetry. Because I plan to contrast this version of a poem with another version in which I sustain the comparison (the metaphor), I keep the two versions similar except for the one difference that I'm highlighting (fleeting versus sustaining references to the metaphor).

line." Again I pointed. "It isn't in the fourth or the fifth line. But here's the thing. I *could* envision a sleeping classroom in more parts of this poem."

Write another version of this poem in front of the children, sustaining the metaphor and thinking aloud as you go.

"So I'm going to try to revise this poem and stay with the idea that the classroom is sleeping, just like Kristine stays with the idea that the tree is like a mother. Okay, listen in as I think aloud. How do I write about coming in to the classroom and talk about the room as if it is sleeping? Hmm, I am remembering when I get to school very early and the classroom is totally quiet. What actions go along with the idea that the classroom is like a sleeping person? Hmm, let me think about what I do when people are sleeping. I know! I tiptoe quietly.

"So now I'll revise my poem to include the things I do that go with the comparison. Instead of saying, 'I come in' I can write 'I tiptoe in quietly.'

"Did you see how I revised that line to include an action that goes with the image of a sleeping person?

I continued in this way, line by line, for the rest of the poem, talking aloud as I made my revisions.

"Okay class, this is the final draft of the poem. Let's read it and see if the image of a sleeping, and then waking, classroom stays across all the lines."

New Version

Mornings
I tiptoe in quietly
The classroom is sleeping.
I slide the chairs and tables into their spots
Careful not to bang them.
The classroom needs its rest.
Then the children clang, clatter, bang in
And wake up the room.

Debrief, quickly listing the steps you took to revise the poem.

"Did you see how I decided to make these revisions? I thought, 'What actions go along with the image of a sleeping person?' I tried to add those actions all through the poem."

The teaching component of the minilesson always employs a method of teaching. In this minilesson, the method is demonstration. In an effective demonstration, the teacher begins at the beginning and proceeds through the sequence of activities step by step (not simply talking about them). It helps to speak your thoughts as the demonstration proceeds, so children can almost look inside your mind and see what's going on.

ACTIVE ENGAGEMENT

Involve the kids in revising a poem you prepared using a different comparison from the chart.

"Let's try to stretch out another comparison together. Let's take this one from our chart: 'We line up like a train.' We *could* write it this way." I pointed to the first version I had prepared.

> We line up like a train
> And go down the hall
> To the lunchroom,
> Where we sit down.

"But we could also try to *stretch out* the way we compare our line of kids to a train. Think about actions that go with the image of a train. Think of what people do with trains or what trains do. Show me a thumb when you have some actions in mind." I gave them a minute to think quietly about trains and then had them work with partners to try out some possible revisions to the poem.

After they'd had time to share their ideas, I called them back together to gather a few ideas for revision.

"We could say we buy tickets." Mason said.

"But we don't buy tickets!" Katherine called out.

"Um. Okay, we could say our teacher says, 'All aboard,' so we line up like a train," Mason responded.

"And chug along to the next stop," Sarah added.

"Where we get gas!" Nina chimed in.

I started to write a new version on the chart paper. "Okay, so far we have this." Alongside the first version, I wrote:

> "All aboard!"
> We line up like a train
> And chug down the hall
> To the next stop,
> Where we fuel up.

"You see how we made the comparison go all the way through the poem? So when people read it, they'll get an image of our class as a train, and they won't lose it. I think a lot of you could try this in your poems today. I'm going to add it to the 'Poetry Decisions that Strengthen Meaning' chart, and I want to remind you that this chart is about things poets can *decide* to do, not things all poets *have* to do. That means you could try something on this chart, keep it if you like it, or change your poem back if you don't. The decision is *yours*."

> ## Poetry Decisions that Strengthen Meaning
>
> **Make Meaning with Images**
> - Use honest, precise words.
> - Show, not tell.
>
> **Make Meaning with Music**
> - Pay attention to line breaks.
> - Use patterns and repetition of sounds, words, and lines.
>
> **Put It All Together**
> - Decide on the mood and bring it out.
> - Compare a feeling or object—or anythig at all—to something else.
> - Stretch out a comparison over many lines.

LINK

Invite students to decide on the day's work, suggesting that some will decide to find poems that have comparisons, and decide whether their comparisons should be stretched out.

"Right now, will you think about what you want to do today? Some of you will probably decide to write a new poem or two. Some of you may still be reading your poems aloud and revising them to make them sound right and to bring out the meaning. I bet some of you will start today looking through your folders to see if you have any poems with comparative language. If you want to do very grown-up work, you can ask yourself if it would make sense to try to stretch out the comparison, like we did here with the sleeping classroom and the train-like line. If you decide to try this today, remember to think about actions that go along with your comparison. Revise your poem to include those actions. Off you go!"

Sustaining an Idea, a Mood, or an Image across a Whole Poem

YOU MAY WANT TO KEEP AN EYE OUT FOR CHILDREN who are ready to learn about sustaining an idea, a mood, or an image across a whole poem. You will almost certainly have some children who are writing very brief underdeveloped poems. A poem such as "Moon," by Klara, just begins to explore an image. And then it stops. (See Figure 10–1.)

Moon

I love when
The moon is full
And a little bit when
The moon is half

FIG. 10–1   Klara begins to explore an image.

MID-WORKSHOP TEACHING
Stretching a Comparison, Using Poets' Eyes

"Poets, look up for a second. Elizabeth has been writing a poem about a dandelion, and she was making some changes when I pulled my chair alongside her. She had been comparing the dandelion to a lollipop and then later to a lion. As she reread, she decided to make every line of her poem compare the dandelion to one thing. So you know what she did? She looked at the dandelion with poets' eyes and decided to focus just on the lion comparison. She wrote each line of her poem with that in mind. This is another way to make your comparison keep going through the whole poem, just like Elizabeth!"

Dandelion
by Elizabeth

It's like a lion
sleeping in the
grass.
Then jumping
up and chasing
a zebra and another
and another
Then getting old
with a gray
mane the hairs
blowing off.

FIG. 10–3   Elizabeth focuses on the lion comparison.

Klara's poem doesn't have a metaphor that can be extended, but it does have an image, and you could easily decide to teach students that sustaining anything across a poem is valuable. During the minilesson, children found actions they could add to a poem to sustain a metaphor. Now you can show children that they can also add actions that allow them to thread an image or a mood across a poem. As we worked together in the small group, Klara thought about the way the moon grows more and less prominent and decided to bring some of that into the poem (see Figure 10–2).

Of course, just as sustaining something can be a goal—whether it is a mood, an image, or a comparison—it can also be a goal for students to learn that they can deliberately make shifts within a poem. Earlier you talked to students about the fact that sometimes in a poem, there is one mood at the start and another at the end. Children can learn about shifts, learning that they can bring shifts in feeling, time of day, color, mood, speed, or metaphor in a poem.

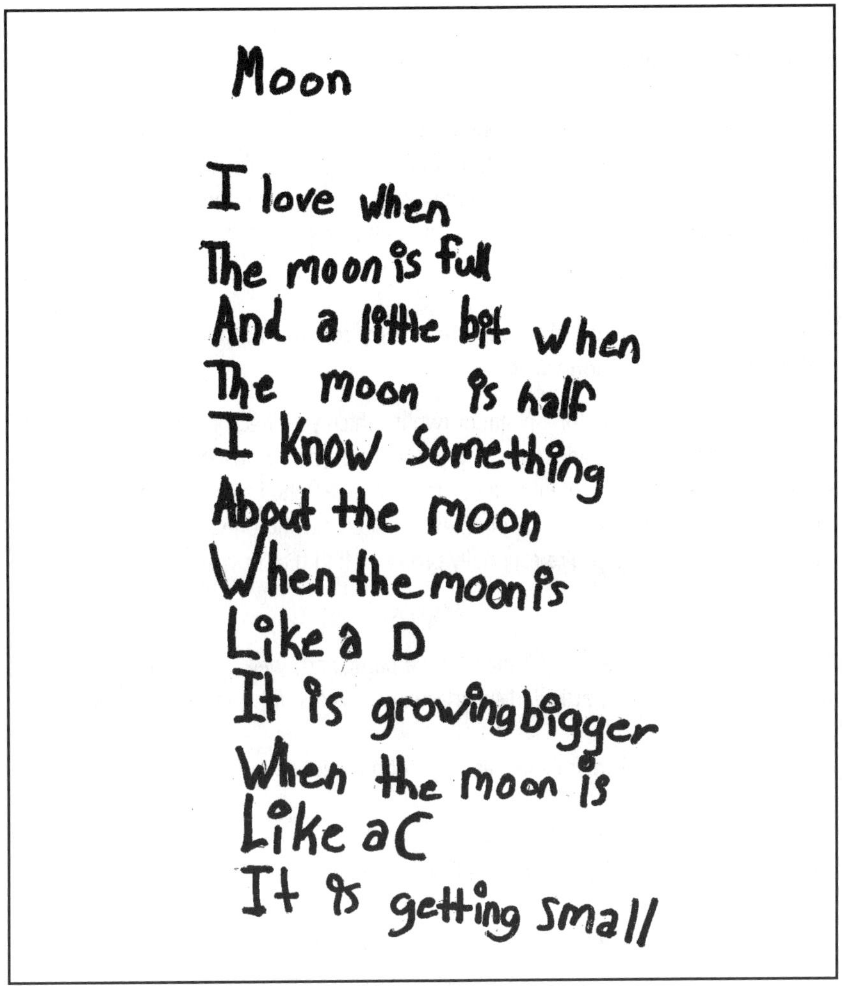

> Moon
>
> I love when
> The moon is full
> And a little bit when
> The moon is half
> I know something
> About the moon
> When the moon is
> Like a D
> It is growing bigger
> When the moon is
> Like a C
> It is getting small

FIG. 10–2 Klara threads an image across her poem.

Reflecting on Learning

Set children up to reflect on what they've learned thus far and to share what they feel they've done particularly well as poets.

"Writers, will you bring your poetry folders with you and join me on the rug?"

Once children were settled, their eyes on me, I said, "Starting tomorrow, we will enter the final stretch of this unit. We're going to be switching gears a bit to focus on another aspect of poetry—structure. That's a way to think about how poems are put together. But, of course, you'll bring all that you've learned up until now with you. So right now, I'd like you to take a moment to reflect on the things you've learned to do with your poets' eyes and ears. Look at our chart, 'Poetry Decisions that Strengthen Meaning,' if you need a reminder."

Ask students to browse their poetry folders, jotting on Post-its® the new ideas they've tried as poets. Ask them to turn and talk with their partners about what they've done well.

I paused briefly, then said, "Now, quickly browse through your folders for a poem or two in which you tried one or two of these things particularly well. You might find you tried out two things in a single poem. Maybe you used precise words that capture just the right image *and* you experimented with line breaks. Or you may have stretched a comparison across your poem *and* used repetition. Or it could be that you've become a bit of an expert at employing one particular poetic technique. Maybe that's your poetry footprint. Whatever it is you're especially proud of, find that now and jot it on a Post-it."

I gave children a couple minutes to mine their folders and take note of what they'd done particularly well. Then I said, "Poets, turn and share with your partner what you've learned to do particularly well across these last few weeks."

The room buzzed while children talked excitedly. I shared some of their examples, highlighting pieces and techniques that reflected true second-grade mastery.

"Writers, in just a few short weeks you have become poetry experts! Tomorrow we'll begin a new exploration phase in this unit, and I know you are ready for it."

We find that it is important to pause and take note of students' hard work as one bend finishes and another begins. There is no need to have over-the-top celebrations at the end of each bend, and in fact, this celebration of growth feels more like a deep breath—an acknowledgment of all that they've done and a gearing up for the more sophisticated learning that is ahead. You need not pull out all the celebration stops at the end of this bend, but we encourage you to take a few moments to recognize how far your students have come.

Studying Structure

IN THIS SESSION, you'll teach students that poets experiment with different structures. In this case, students will study two mentor poems with different structures (a conversation poem and a list poem) and add these structures to their repertoire.

GETTING READY

✔ Chart from Bend I, "Strategies Poets Use to Write Poems" (see Connection)

✔ Tiny Topics notepads (see Connection)

✔ "Maples in October" by Amy Ludwig VanDerwater, written on chart paper (see Teaching and Active Engagement)

✔ "Destiny" by Kristine O'Connell George, written on chart paper and one copy for each student in their poetry folders (see Teaching and Active Engagement)

✔ Bags of assorted items (rocks, spoons, clay, and so on) from which children will make various things (see Share)

✔ You may also want to stock folders with poems (which you have permission to copy) written in a variety of structures that you hope students will notice and emulate. See the online resources for sample poems by Amy Ludwig VanDerwater and Zoë Ryder White. See also Amy's blog, http://www.poem-farm.amylv.com/, an excellent resource of both poems and poetry ideas.

AS STUDENTS VENTURE INTO THE THIRD BEND of this unit, you will help them focus on structure—sometimes also referred to as form, organization, or design—and on the ways structure relates to the sounds and the meaning of poetry. In a poem, structure is especially visible. The words stand on one page, and even just a look at that page reveals something about a poem's structure. The lines of one poem alternate between two voices. The lines of another are jagged and short, until the poem's end when the words cascade, one after another after another, a long single line.

Of course, your children won't be very skilled at talking about the structures of poetry. They are not apt to come to this unit knowing the domain-specific vocabulary for talking about poems (or, in fact, for *thinking* about poems), so you will want to provide them with some of that language and some of the accompanying concepts. Children can learn that just as there are prose genres—mysteries, fables, historical fiction, personal narrative—so, too, are there kinds of poems. More than this, they will learn that poets can "try on" those different kinds of poems. Just as a sculptor molds a piece of clay this way and that, manipulating it until it takes on a form that seems right, so, too, a writer plays with the words and sentences on a page until she finds a form that best fits what she hopes to say.

Poets make a design, a structure, with words, information, and ideas. Today's session will teach children that as poets, they can take a topic, and they can think about that topic one way and then another way. By exploring a variety of structures, youngsters can learn that the palette a writer draws upon contains not just ideas, experiences, and language; it also contains structures. They'll learn this, above all, from being invited to explore poetic structures. They will emulate their favorite authors and mimic poetic forms. Tomorrow you will teach into this work more explicitly, guiding children through an inquiry in which they'll name the component parts of various poetic forms. Today, simply draw your children's attention to the idea of different structures, and let them play.

Studying Structure

CONNECTION

◆ COACHING

Rally children's energy for this final and most sophisticated bend in the road. Remind them of all they know about choosing a topic for a poem, and ask them to choose one.

"Poets, will you join me in the meeting area?" I asked, and once they were settled, I began. "Today begins the final bend in our poetry unit. You've learned so much about writing poetry already, and now I think you are ready to dive into even more sophisticated ideas. How many of you have ever been on a roller coaster?" The children signaled, and most had. "You know that feeling when you're poised at the top of the hill, and you can see the land all around you? And then the car slowly starts to creep toward the edge, and suddenly, you're flying! Writing poetry can feel like that. We're all together on a roller coaster, ready to start this next bend, and before we do, we must climb up, up, up, and that will take some work. Ready?

"So, you've already been watching the world with poets' eyes, and you are probably already brimming with ideas for new poems. You can always use our chart to help you get started, too, if you're stuck."

You'll be instilling a bit of drama, hyping the upcoming bend in the unit, and meanwhile continuing the theme in this series of valuing the opportunity to work hard. Strong writing grows in the soil of hard work.

Strategies Poets Use to Write Poems

- Poets find a big topic that gives them a big feeling.
- Poets find a small moment, detail, or object that holds the big feeling.
- Poets look with poets' eyes and see this ordinary thing in a new way.
- Poets write about it, experimenting with line breaks.

"Before we dig into today's new work, right this second, think of a topic you really know and care about so you can write a poem about that topic today. You can flip through your Tiny Topics notepads or just think of a poem idea that's been on your mind lately." I gave the children a minute to think and then asked them to signal with a thumbs-up when they had decided on an idea. "Once you have your idea, turn and tell your partner what you'll write a poem about today." The room erupted, and I listened in as children shared their new ideas.

Because we want students to be able to really focus on the new ideas, it helps for them to already have a topic in mind before we launch into the next part of the lesson. But keep this quick. The meat of the lesson is to come.

Explain to children that one thing (whether an object or an idea for a poem) can take on many different structures.

Gathering the class, I said, "Keep your idea in mind. I promise we'll get back to it. So, one of my favorite things to do is take long walks on the beach collecting shells. I walk until my bucket is practically overflowing and then head home. Then I take out my shells, one by one, and lay them on the floor. When they are all there, I always ask myself, 'What should I do with these shells this time? What will they become?'

"One year I decided to string them together. I used colorful yarn and made necklaces and bracelets out of those shells, lots of them, for all my friends. Another year I turned the shells into little creatures. I would choose small shells that could become heads and glued them onto bigger shells, for bodies, and glued on feet, too. I made turtles and crabs and a mother cat with little kittens around her, all from shells. One year, I filled a glass lamp with my shells.

"Now, here's where your poem idea comes back in: just as shells can become many things—a necklace, a turtle, the filled in lamp—the topic you've chosen can be shaped in different ways. And each of those different shapes can still be a poem. I'm sure you've realized that poems do *not* all look or sound the same. Poems are built in different shapes—or as poets would say, they have different structures."

❧ Name the teaching point.

"Today I want to teach you that when a poet writes a poem, the poet experiments with different structures. To do this, the poet studies what other authors have done and then tries those different structures on for size."

TEACHING AND ACTIVE ENGAGEMENT

Teach by guided practice. You'll be walking kids step by step through the process of thinking of a topic, then considering several structures, then trying them on.

"So, first, the poet has something to say. Right now, will you hold your topic in your hands?" I cupped my hands to show that I was holding my topic. "I'm holding my topic now. It's about cooking chili with my brother."

"Now, in your own mind, think of some words you might put into a poem about *your* topic. Get some jottings going in your mind, jottings that could become a poem later."

I looked intently at the invisible topic in my own hands and started whispering some words about it. "Cans of beans, spices, smooshed tomatoes." The children were doing the same with their own topics.

These questions—What do I have? What can I make?—are questions that poets ask themselves over and over. By sharing this shell story, you help children understand that like shells, lines for poems lie everywhere. Throughout this unit, you might notice such lines across the day. "Look! A poem line!"

When you are teaching a concept to kids, it is important to come up with a very short list of the terms that you'll treat as synonyms. In this instance, we're using "shapes" and "structures" as synonyms. We could also use the term forms, *but it is probably best to not throw around too many terms until kids grasp the primary ones we are using.*

Notice this is both teaching and engagement—we'll cycle through these twice.

When you model getting lost in your own work in this way, students have an opportunity to observe and learn from your writing process, to see that you are not distracted by their side conversations, so interested are you in writing. As teachers of writing, we are always modeling process and work habits as well as specific writing strategies.

Reveal a poem with a very distinct text structure, and ask children to annotate it with their observations. Set two kids up to do so at the easel while others work at their rugs spots.

"Now that you've got your minds around your ideas, think about possible structures in which your poem might be written. (Structure just means the specific way a poem is put together). Let's just look at a few possibilities for now. Let's look at one kind of structure first and notice what the poet, Amy, has done to organize, to put together, her poem."

I read the first poem, which was written on chart paper, accentuating the alternating lines representing alternating voices.

Maples in October
by Amy Ludwig VanDerwater

They rustle to each other—

I think today's the day.
  Wind is getting colder.
Geese are on their way.
  Oak is throwing acorns.
It's time to go ahead.
  I think today's the day.
Let's change our leaves to red.

"If you could jot what you notice about how that poem goes, what would you jot?" I added, "In the air, jot what you notice as though you are writing right there in the margins of the poem. That's what poets do. It's called *annotating* the poem. We'll *actually* annotate the one on chart paper up here." I signaled to Silas and Claire to come to the easel and gave them each a marker. I took one as well, and while they annotated the poem, I added a label to the whole project: "Annotating the poem." While they worked at the easel, the other children wrote-in-the-air at their rug spots. Silas jotted, "This guy is talking to that guy," with arrows to the alternating lines. Claire recorded that this was a conversation, and they were talking about fall.

After a quick survey of the kids working on the rug, I continued. "So, here is the important thing. Poets think about their topic and think about a structure. Shall we call this one a conversation poem? Hmm. Might this structure be right for your topic? Let me think, too, might a conversation poem be right for my poem about making chili with my brother? Don't decide yet! Just keep it in your mind!"

You may wonder about using a term like anno-tate with second-graders, but the truth is, this word has a very concrete and clear meaning, and it is something you are asking kids to do. They'll relish being given the technical term and will feel very grown-up. You won't just be teaching them the specific term; you'll be teaching them that experts on a topic learn the lingo of that topic.

You might decide to have children come up with their own names for the structures you introduce.

Channel children to annotate a second poem, one with a contrasting and distinct structure, again thinking of this structure as a possibility for their intended poems.

"Let's look at a second poem." I displayed the second poem on the easel, next to the first.

Destiny
by Kristine O'Connell George

Some trees will become
    Grandfather Clocks
    Carousel Horses
    Grand Pianos
    Podiums or Front Porches
    Totem Poles
    or Cathedral Doors with Intricate Latches.

Others, pencils, toothpicks, or ordinary kitchen matches.

"This one is in your folder. Quick, take it out and annotate it. Jot your observations in the margins, and I'll be doing the same." I began annotating the poem on the easel and gestured for Claire and Silas to continue as well. As the children worked on their poems, I voiced over, "Notice the structure, the way the whole thing is organized. That's the part we are thinking about right now. Is this a conversation poem too? If not, how would you describe it?"

On the chart, Silas jotted, "It's all the things trees become."

I quietly said to him, "Yes, it's like a list of all the things trees become." Then I looked at his note and added, "You better put in that it is a *list* of the things trees become, right?" He nodded and inserted that into his note.

I called the children back together. "Poets, I can see that many of you are saying that this poem is not a conversation. It's a list. Kristine doesn't list the things she wants for her birthday or the things she will buy at the grocery store. She lists all the things that trees become, listing one after the other after the other. Hmm, a list poem. That's another structure poets sometimes use."

Remind students that poets experiment with alternative structures. Recruit the class to help you imagine your topic in one of these structures.

"Poets, you looked at only two poems today, but already you noticed that sometimes poets write conversation poems—where one person or object talks to another—and sometimes they write list poems. When poets write, they make decisions about what structure their poems will take. Will you help me try it out with my chili poem, right now? Let's see. This would probably work in either structure, but let's try a conversation poem first.

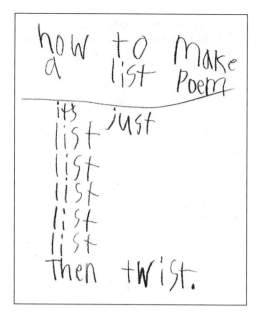

FIG. 11–1 West's "How to Make a List" poem

Be on the lookout for list poems to share with your class; you will find many. It is one of the most common structures for poems and one of the easiest for children to try. Both of the structures you introduce today are ones your students will recognize if they peruse anthologies of poems. You might invite them to "treasure hunt" for the new structures you study and share their findings with the class.

Later, West wrote a how-to list poem (see Figure 11–1) linked to today's teaching. It is easy to find procedural poems such as this one in children's anthologies, and your students may choose to add a category of "how-to poems" to your class poetry wall. "How to Talk to Your Snowman" by Beverly McLoughland and Eve Merriam's "How to Eat a Poem" are two such examples.

"What could I do to start a conversation poem about making chili with my brother? Talk to each other. How could I start? Who's talking?"

I listened in and asked students to share ideas. Culling from what I'd heard, I'd soon written the beginnings of a conversation poem on chart paper.

> I'll read the recipe.
> I'll open the cans.
> Don't forget the garlic.

"Let's stop for now. You've given me a great start! Later, I'll finish this poem, or maybe I'll try making a list poem."

Debrief to point out the replicable steps you just helped the class to do.

"Writers, the work you are doing is work that poets do all the time. Poets often start with a topic, with something to say, and then they try putting that topic into one structure and then another. Sometimes, they don't just try one way that a conversation poem could go, or a list poem. They try a bunch of ways. This is how poets find the structure that seems to be the best fit for what they want to say."

LINK

With their chosen topic in mind, channel students to consider different ways to build a poem around that topic, using different structures. Once you see a child writing, send that child off to work at his or her seat.

"Will you, again, hold your poem idea in your hands. Now, without thinking about structure, say some words, some images, that might go in your poem. Say these to yourself, in a whisper or silently." I waited for children to do that and coached into what a few of them were doing.

"Now the hard part. As you keep thinking about and saying words and images that could go into your poem, think, 'So what ideas am I beginning to get for how I could turn this into a list poem or a conversation poem or some other structure that we haven't talked about yet?'" I again left time for children to do this alone.

"Today when you go off to write, first open your folders and read through your mentor poems, jotting what you notice about how the poems are structured. Is one poem a list? Can you find a poem that goes back and forth or repeats certain lines or images? What new things will you notice about how poets organize, or structure, their poems? Begin your writing work today by reading, annotating the poems in your folder, and allowing them to give you new ideas for structuring your own poems. Then, let your reading lead you right into writing poems of your own. You might try writing the same idea in two different structures! Poets do that all the time."

I don't want to take too much time with this now, so I make a mental note to come back and finish the poem later.

Poems Have Structures

- **Conversation poems** include two voices—"Maples in October"
- **List poems** are lists—"Destiny"

We suggest getting students started this way because it can be easier to think about structure when there has already been a bit of language generated around a topic.

You are coaching the children to do some ambitious work. They won't all be able to do this, just now in the minilesson. That's okay. You'll be able to help them during the workshop itself.

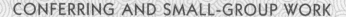
Help Students Read Poems Attentively

TODAY'S WRITING TIME will progress from reading and annotating poems to writing poems. As your students pick up poems to read on their own, you'll want to use every possible opportunity to mentor them in this work. This may surprise you. You may think, "Early on in today's workshop, they won't be writing yet. Does reading a poem really take so much mentorship?" But the truth is that your demonstrations can make it vastly more likely that your children actually engage in close reading. If you listen attentively to their conversations and to the poems they are responding to, you can show a level of attentiveness to and respect for the text that will quickly rub off on your students. Let the poems give you goose bumps, let them make you gasp and laugh and marvel and peer more closely at the page. Be astonished. And bring the youngsters in on your responsive, wide-awake reading.

After you help children read well, responding deeply to the poems, then it will be a natural extension for you to help children turn around in their tracks and ask, "How did the author do that?" "How did she make me laugh aloud?" "What did she do to make me stop at this part and read it again and marvel?" World-class standards ask you to nudge students to go a step further and also ask, "Why might she have done this? How do the decisions she made about craft reflect the themes she's putting forward in the poem?"

By helping students think about the decisions that an author has made, you will be continuing a long-standing effort to help your children understand that there are real people behind texts, and those real people have made choices between this structure and that one, this word and that one, this ending and that one. As you engage with children's work, use poets' names. Help them be on a first-name basis with poets. Ask questions such as, "What do you see that Joyce did in this poem? How did Kristine decide to structure her stanzas?" Then help them turn this observation into possibilities for their own work by asking, "What are you learning from Patrick that you plan to try in your own poem today?"

MID-WORKSHOP TEACHING   New Goals for Writing

"Poets, can I stop you?" I said. "You've done some really nice work. Right now, if you are wearing green, will you stand up?" Around the room, children stood up, giggling a little at this strange command. "Those of you wearing green, will you show the kids who are near you what you wrote today? I'm guessing that lots of you tried out writing your poem using one, or maybe even both, of the structures we studied. Go!"

After the children talked and shared for a bit, I said, "Now, those of you who aren't wearing green today, stand up. What did you just learn that could help your poetry? If your mind was turned on full force while you were helping Mr. or Miss Green, I'm very sure *you* learned something even while you were helping. I'm very sure you can come up with some idea for how you can make your poems better—the one you worked on today and others. So right now, think of what ideas you have for how your poems could be improved." I gave them a long moment of silence—one that felt especially long because they were still standing. "Thumbs up if you thought of a way to improve your poems." They all gestured so.

"So we just have fifteen more minutes, and you have a lot of work to do. I bet you'll be revising your poems. And also, don't forget, in addition to looking at the structure of the poems in your folder, try annotating one with a few different cool things that you notice. Then take the same poem idea, and try writing it in the structure that you have just studied."

Using Manipulatives to Think about Structure

Distribute bags full of assorted items, and channel tables of kids to make something out of the stuff. Then channel them to use the same stuff to make something different and, finally, to discuss how that work relates to the teaching point of the day.

"Poets, get to your seats. We're not going to come together for today's share." The children moved to their seats. Then I distributed a bag of stuff to each table, with the strictest instructions *not* to open the bag until I gave the word. The bags contained items that could be combined to make creatures, castles, tea parties: rocks, shells, clay, feathers, a few spoons. I'd collected the items with thoughts in mind for several alternative things that these could easily become. "Poets, you have three minutes. Work together to make the contents of your bag into something that you care about. Go!"

After a minute and a half, I said, "One more minute," and then, shortly thereafter, I stopped the children and asked them to stand back so they could see each other's creations. There were a lot of arched necks, and then I said, "Here is the hard part. You have two minutes to make something altogether different. Go!" After a flurry of energy, I stopped them, and this time said, "Here is the important question. What does this activity have to do with poetry? Talk together about that."

I listened in as children climbed onto their knees in excitement, trying to put into words the teaching point of the day.

Debrief, leaving students with the take-away that you hope they will remember as they continue writing and revising their poems.

"Poets, I can see that each table group has made such a different thing from your treasure bag. Table 1 has made a chicken picture from their items and table 2 has made a bicycle. From the same materials, you have imagined so many possibilities. This is just what poets do; they shape their ideas into all kinds of structures, over and over again, all through their lives."

This kinetic activity will get the attention of students who learn best that way. In addition to illustrating your teaching point about structure, the activity itself is a kind of metaphor. You will want to listen carefully to what students say as they ponder the ways this activity relates to writing poetry, and of course, you may decide to seed the conversation if you feel they are not grasping your point.

Close Reading of a Mentor Text

IN THIS SESSION, you'll teach students that poets often study other poems to learn about how they are structured, and they try out those new structures in their own poems.

GETTING READY

✔ "Maples in October" by Amy Ludwig VanDerwater, written on chart paper (see Teaching)

✔ "Reading a Poem with Poets' Eyes" chart, with first bullet prewritten (see Teaching)

✔ Your own writing folder

✔ Space on the poetry wall or poetry bulletin board for children to share their work (see Link)

✔ Student folders filled with mentor poems in a variety of structures (see Link)

✔ For the sample conference, we used Kristine O'Connell George's poem "Fly Fishing in Crystal River" as an example of a story poem. You may want to have the mentor text, *Old Elm Speaks*, with you as you confer today.

✔ Legos to show children how they might represent the structure of poems using different colored legos and connecting them in different ways (see Conferring)

TEACHERS. Pause in your reading and look around you. Now look again, and this time, look with the eyes of a poet.

My expectation is that when you read that command—"Look with the eyes of a poet"—you opened your eyes in a different kind of way. You didn't just scan the room; you actually looked. You took in detail that usually glides past you. You saw, thought, wondered, questioned. That mental alertness—that's a big deal.

You'll recall that this entire unit started with you asking children to use poets' eyes to look, and to really see, objects that you'd brought into the room. You talked early on in this unit about the difference between seeing with ordinary eyes and seeing with a poets' eyes. Your children have learned that they can pick up a leaf and see each vein of it. They can see each ripple on a moth's wing and note the fairy dust.

Today you will suggest that your youngsters need to bring that same mental alertness, that same attentiveness to detail, to their work studying the texts that other authors have written. They can see those texts as they see the wing of the moth: with wide-eyed attentiveness. You'll teach children that poets use their poets' eyes to study mentor texts. They notice things others would pass by. And they do not just notice; they think. They see patterns, they see surprises, they wonder, they question.

And because the poets are studying the texts to make reading-writing connections, they also ask that question that your youngsters will have asked for years now: "What has this writer done that I could try?" Because they are especially studying structure, you will channel children to also ask, "How does this sort of writing go? What is the 'recipe' the writer used to create this sort of writing?"

Yesterday children mentored themselves to poems in somewhat cursory ways—reading for the gist of how a poem goes and then maybe trying out only two different structures. Today you will focus their attention more closely on structure. It is work that will serve your children well whenever they read and write.

This work alone could fill a minilesson to its brim, but you start by teaching children that when making something, it can help to borrow the form that someone else has used, sometimes following that form, sometimes improvising off it. Although many people think of poets as ultra-creative rule breakers (after all, they aren't held to the same conventions for punctuation and capitals), the truth is that poets often work within existing forms. The power of poetry, then, comes not just from trying to put something too big for words into a small number of carefully chosen words, but also from trying to put something nebulous into a very defined form. Often those forms exist before the poet even begins to write, and sometimes the form is one the poet makes as he or she writes.

In any case, you'll begin this session by teaching that poets think about the steps for making poems in one structure or another.

"Teach children that poets use their poets' eyes to study mentor texts—to notice things others would pass by."

Close Reading of a Mentor Text

CONNECTION

Remind writers that the content of a poem can go into one structure or another.

"Writers, you've been thinking about the way that poets try out—you could say, follow—different possible structures. Yesterday, many of you tried to put your content into a conversation poem, a list poem, and into other kinds of poems as well.

"Really, what you have been doing is what writers do all the time. A writer has something to say. For example, I have something to say about cooking chili with my brother. I can write that content as a letter to my brother or as a fiction story that might revolve around a girl who learns to cook with her brother (or her cousin, even, since fiction needn't follow real life). Or that day of cooking with my brother could become a persuasive speech. We had to convince our parents to let us cook by delivering a speech that said, 'We are responsible enough to cook for this reason, this reason, this reason.'

"The thing is that if I was writing this content in a letter, I'd need to follow the rules—the recipe, almost—for a letter. I'd need to think, 'What will my letter need to contain?'"

The children called out that I'd need to start, "Dear . . . " and to end, "Your sister . . . " or something similar.

Explain to children that when they want to emulate anything—a form of writing, an activity, a process—it helps to study that thing closely and attempt to name its component parts.

"Now, I could ask you what my writing would need to contain if it was a poem, but my point today is that the answer is a bit different depending on the kind of poem (or the poem structure) that I am writing. If my poem is a conversation poem, what will I need? Thumbs up if you have an idea." The children signaled and said that two voices would need to be talking for a conversation poem. In the same way, students shared what would go into a list poem.

This talk about how one topic can be recast in a variety of ways helps students understand that the content of their writing is pliable and can be reused, reshaped into different genres and structures. Such talk will also lay a foundation for the children's work next year and beyond, when they will keep writer's notebooks, mining them for topics that can be rewritten in different ways.

❖ **Name the teaching point.**

"Today I want to teach you that because poets think, 'What kind of structure will work for what I have to say?' they become experts on different kinds of writing. To do this, poets study the structures that other poets use just like they study feathers and stones. They see details and wonder, connect, question."

TEACHING

Remind children that one way to revise poetry is by studying mentor poems.

"Sometimes poets study mentor poems to get ideas for revising their own poems, and I want to teach you one way to do that. Right now, hold your right hand out in front of you and look at it with ordinary eyes. Tell your partner what you see." The children did this, each noting they saw a hand and they saw five fingers. "Now, writers, look at your right hand again, and this time, look with a poets' eyes." I gave them a minute of silence in which to do that and meanwhile peered at the cracks and veins in my own hand. Then I said, "Tell your partner what you see now, when looking with a poets' eyes."

I listened to the kids' conversations, coaching them to reach for precise words and to use comparisons to say more. After listening for a bit, I said, "Writers, you have gone from saying, 'I see five fingers' to saying, 'My hand has lots of wrinkles and lines all over it. I can read it like I read a map.' Amazing what you see when you see with a poets' eyes!"

Demonstrate reading a poem with the eyes of a poet, noticing details. Alternate between reading and pausing to name what the poet has done.

"Today I want to point out that poets study *poems* with poets' eyes. Let's study this poem, "Maples in October," as poets do, with poets' eyes. This time, see if you can name *exactly* what Amy does." I began to read the poem aloud, visibly grappling with the question. I paused after the third line.

> Maples in October
> by Amy Ludwig VanDerwater
>
> They rustle to each other—
>
> *I think today's the day.*
>   Wind is getting colder.

After the first three lines. I repeated the opening line. "'They rustle to each other.' I'm not totally sure what rustling to each other means, but the word *rustling* sounds like the leaves when the wind makes them shake and scrape together. And she says they rustle *to each other*. She's personifying the trees, isn't she? She's making it seem that they are people, murmuring to each other." I jotted "personifies" in the margin, annotating the poem.

The structures that your students come to understand through poetry are structures they have encountered before and will encounter again in other genres. This bigger teaching, that poets study the structures that other poets use, is more important than the structures themselves.

"Looking with poets' eyes" is a phrase you may choose to weave throughout your school day and year. Poets study the world closely, looking for connections and meaning, and this way of seeing should not be restricted to one unit of study. Learning to see with different kinds of eyes (poets' eyes, scientists' eyes, writers' eyes) opens possibilities for young children across disciplines.

When children see the whole poem, they'll see it has a dialogic back-and-forth structure.

By using technical words like personification *and defining the word right afterward ("making it seem as if they are people"), you welcome students into the language of professional writers.*

Then I stopped and said, "Are you noticing some things about how I read a poem with my poets' eyes? Think about *how* I am reading this poem. Could you do this same kind of reading?" I flipped over the chart paper, showing the beginning of a chart.

> ### Reading a Poem with Poets' Eyes
>
> - Read it really slowly, noticing and naming details you see.

Demonstrate that poets notice what the author has done and ask why the author has done that. Then they consider doing the same thing.

Then I said, "Here's what I do next. Watch." Then I looked at the poem and said, "Why might the author have done this? Why might Amy have started her poem by making her trees talk to each other?" I looked over the poem and then said, "Maybe she's trying to make the trees come to life and to get us to think about what trees might say—and think about—if they were like people.

"Poets, now watch." I then looked at my own writing folder and said, "I wonder if I could try some of the things Amy did in her poem?"

I jotted the final two bullets on the new class chart.

> ### Reading a Poem with Poets' Eyes
>
> - Read it really slowly, noticing and naming details you see.
> - Ask, "Why might the poet have decided to write like this?" Answer this too.
> - Try borrowing some of the same techniques, using them in your poem.

Although the focus of this portion of the unit is a reading to notice how authors structure poems, you are really looking at all the tiny decisions authors make that relate to the larger structured decisions. So notice any unusual features or language.

ACTIVE ENGAGEMENT

Give children an opportunity to try the same techniques on the next few lines of the same poem.

"Will you read just a tiny bit more, reading slowly, noticing and naming details that you see?" I gestured to the chart as I spoke. "After you spot something, ask, '*Why* might the author have decided to write like this?' Work with partners. This will be hard work, so seat belts on!"

> *Geese are on their way.*
> Oak is throwing acorns.
> *It's time to go ahead.*
> I think today's the day.
> *Let's change our leaves to red.*

The children talked and I listened. John said, "I notice she has different guys, I mean trees, talking. She skips lines to show which guy is talking."

Convene the writers, highlight what they have said, and channel them to imagine doing similar work in their own writing.

After a minute, I reconvened the writers. "Writers, can I have your attention? Holy moly. You said some really interesting things. Some of you noticed that Amy changed the way the lines look so you know who is talking, and she indents too.

"Right now, will you think about a conversation poem you wrote yesterday or the one you might write today? And think whether you could try some of the things Amy has done, like personification or using the structure of the poem to show who is talking to whom."

LINK

Channel students to continue studying and annotating this poem, and others, emulating what they notice as they revise the poems they wrote the previous day and write more.

"Poets, we've just studied the very start of this one poem. Today I'm pretty sure many of you will want to use your poets' eyes to find lots of other little moves that you didn't see the first time you read your mentor poems. And you'll revise your poems. Jerry pointed out that there is still space on our mentor poetry board, so if you rewrite one of your poems and you are really proud of it, see me and we'll make a space for it.

"Remember, poets often annotate poems they are studying—mark them up and leave marginal notes—to help keep track of what they are thinking as they read. If you do that work today, you'll notice that as you get started revising or writing your own poems, you'll be working differently because of all that you noticed!"

For more about reading texts like writers in this way, read Wondrous Words *by Katie Wood Ray.*

By naming the very specific moves that a poet makes, you forge a clear path for students to not only try these particular moves, but for them to notice such moves themselves.

You may want to hang the conversation poems together, the list poems together, the story poems together, and so on. Before long, your students will be finding these structures in poetry books on their own, exclaiming, "Look! Another conversation poem! Let's put it on the board!"

Using Small Groups to Teach a Variety of Structures

BEFORE YOU BEGIN CONFERRING and leading small groups today, you'll want to think about whether you want to recruit a small group to explore a topic you'll eventually share with the class. You could then use the small group to teach the class. This is a very powerful way to channel information to the class, because of course, it is exciting for the small group of children to try something utterly new, and it is even more exciting for them to share their work with the rest of the class.

For example, you will probably be hankering to populate the classroom with a few more kinds of poems. We decided that instead of teaching yet more structures, it would be better to teach students to study poems themselves to discern their structures. But because we had a few structures we thought would be especially helpful, we decided to "seed" the class by providing poems with those structures to members of a small group.

For example, I knew that I wanted students to give story poems a try. When I noticed Sally studying Kristine O'Connell George's poem "Fly Fishing in the Crystal River," I gathered a few other likely candidates to join in a study of that poem and its structure. I suggested I'd read the poem, then they could read it in pairs to each other, and then they might take some time to annotate it silently before comparing notes and thoughts.

Fly Fishing in the Crystal River
by Kristine O'Connell George

I hitch up my waders
step into the cold river
let out some line
gather up the slack
pull my rod back
snap my wrist
and catch
  a pine

Elizabeth began, "She is telling about a time she went fishing." I gestured for her to add on. "It's kind of like a story of fishing. Only it's not like a story exactly . . . because it's poem-y."

MID-WORKSHOP TEACHING

Spreading New Small-Group Learning across the Class

"Oh my gosh, poets. Eyes up here." I waited. "You all are inventing a lot of knowledge. Ben, can you tell the class some of what you have discovered about story poems?"

As Ben talked about story poems, I revealed the list we had written on chart paper and then attached this and Kristine's "Fly Fishing in Crystal River" poem to our mentor poetry board.

Writing a Story Poem
- Tell a story bit by bit.
- Focus on a small moment.
- Add detail.
- Spice it up with strong words.

"Poets, let's use this board as a place to record new poetry structures. Then you can hang mentor poems and your own poems here too." I pointed out that there was now a display of conversation poems, list poems, and story poems. "I cannot wait to see what other new structures you discover."

I asked, "What *exactly* did Kristine do to tell the story of the time she went fishing?"

"Well," said Ban, "she told all the little parts of the story, kinda bit by bit like we do in small moments." After a bit more discussion of how what they knew about writing Small Moment stories could help them write story poems, we compiled the following plan for writing a story poem.

Writing a Story Poem
- Tell a story bit by bit.
- Focus on a small moment.
- Add detail.
- Spice it up with strong words.

I reminded students that poets often try writing the same content in a variety of structures and told them that since they had just "discovered" a new structure, the story poem, they might want to try it out, using their poem topics from the day before. I explained that while this structure wouldn't work for everyone or for every topic, it would for many.

I gathered another small group of children together who had tried list poems, and I suggested they might study ways that poets tend to end their poems. "Something interesting about list poems," I confided, "is that they often have a special kind of ending, a twist ending."

I asked Carolyn to share her stuffed animal poem with this group. In the poem, she'd listed all of the animals and ended with "They've known me forever." I pointed out, "Can you see how Carolyn's poem talks about one animal, another animal, another animal, another animal, then a feeling? She breaks the pattern at the end. She adds a twist. That's what list poems do." I reached into my pocket and pulled out ten snapped together Legos: all green but for one red at the bottom. "See how the pattern changes at the end of this tower? Poems can have patterns, just like Lego structures do, and sometimes the pattern breaks at the end and surprises us."

You might carry a pocketful of Legos, inviting children to try representing the organization of various poems, directing their attention specifically to structure.

Poems Have Structures
- **Conversation poems** include two voices—"Maples in October"
- **List poems** are lists—"Destiny"
- **Story poems** tell about moments, bit-by-bit—"Fly fishing in the Crystal River"

Partners Celebrate Structures

Ask children to reflect on their work and their mentors and share with a partner.

"Writers, we have looked at stones and leaves and flowers with poets' eyes, and I can hear from your conversations that you are even looking at your own poems with poets' eyes, too. It is exciting to see you asking, 'What kind of poem will match my topic?'

"Quickly look over the poem or poems that you wrote today and think of some words to describe how you decided to organize your poem." I gave children a minute to do this. "Will you think if there is a mentor poem that has helped you write your poem?" Again I gave children time to think about this.

"Partner 1, will you read your poem aloud to Partner 2, and then will you talk about which poet helped you write your poem today? What did you learn from that poet? Listen carefully to each other because I am sure that you will each get new ideas for things to try in your own poems tomorrow!"

Matching Structures to Feelings

R OBERT FROST'S WORDS "No tears in the writer, no tears in the reader" are often quoted in books about poetry. Poetry seeks to stir feelings in readers, and poets experiment with a variety of structures to convey moods and feelings. Specifically, poets ask themselves, "What do I hope my reader feels or experiences when reading this poem?" and "What structure will get readers to feel that way?"

Look through any children's magazine and you will see topics that are written about in more than one genre. Perhaps you'll find both a story and a procedural article about building a bird feeder with Grandpa. When you read the story about building a bird feeder, you feel nostalgic. And when you read the how-to article about the bird feeder, you feel ready to work. Structure choices are intentional.

IN THIS SESSION, you'll teach students that there is a relationship between structure and meaning in poetry. Poets choose a structure that is the right fit for what they want to say.

GETTING READY

✔ With permission, the work of a child, selected in advance to model what to do when a selected form doesn't bring out one's intended meaning. This could be a fictional child from a prior year of teaching or one from your current class if the occasion arises (see Connection and Active Engagement).

✔ Two teacher-written poems, on chart paper, each written about the same topic but in a different structure (see Teaching)

"No tears in the writer, no tears in the reader."

Today your larger message will be that poets use structure to convey meaning. Your observations will help children understand that structure is a choice—a choice that makes a reader think and feel in certain ways.

This session builds off of the work children did in Bend II, when they learned how to use the two main elements of poetry—sound and language—to give their poems meaning. Today, you'll return to the notion that poets, like all writers, use everything they can to bring out meaning.

Matching Structures to Feelings

CONNECTION

Tell the story of a child who wrote a poem and decided its structure didn't match its meaning.

"Poets, you've spent the past couple days experimenting with different structures for poems. You've written conversation poems, list poems, and story poems.

"Yesterday, Henry looked a little perplexed as he was writing, so I pulled up a chair and asked him what was going on. He'd been writing about his dog, and he had a poem that went like this."

> Fetch a stick
> Chew a bone
> Bark at cars
> Roll over
> Lick people
> Sit and stay
> Be a dog

"I thought it was a terrific list poem until Henry pointed out his problem. He said, 'It doesn't work. I wanted it to show that Tucker can do amazing tricks! Like about the time he learned to roll over, on his back, with his legs up.' I realized what he meant. The list form Henry used shows lots of actions—but it doesn't show a lot about any one trick. It doesn't tell about 'a moment when . . .'

"That got me thinking. Poets don't just try any ol' structure. They think really hard about what kind of poem is going to be best for what they want to say. And specifically, they think about what kind of poem will give readers the feeling, the mood, the meaning they want readers to get."

◆ COACHING

If you have made a class bulletin board to highlight these structures, you might direct students' attention here, inviting them to add their own poems in the proper section.

Look for opportunities to help students understand that structure and words are always at the service of meaning. Rather than, "pick a structure, find an idea," writers "choose a meaningful topic, match a structure to it."

❖ **Name the teaching point.**

"Today I want to teach you that poets ask themselves, 'What do I hope my reader feels when reading this poem?' and then they try to make sure that they choose a structure for their poem that gets readers to feel what they want them to feel, to think what they want them to think."

TEACHING

Examine a poem you wrote in several forms, considering which best conveys your intended meaning.

"Let me show you what I mean. I've been trying on different structures, different kinds of poetry, for the idea about cooking chili with my brother. I've written a list poem, a conversation poem, and I could write a story poem too. It is sort of like I have been trying on all those different structures for size—like I could try on some different shirts for size. But now, I think I need to start asking whether one of those structures fits or not. And to figure out if a structure fits or not, I need to think about whether it makes readers feel what I want them to feel."

"Hmm, what *do* I hope a reader will feel when reading this poem?

"Hmm, I think want my reader to know that my brother and I were really helping each other, working side by side, together. So let me see which form gives that feeling especially." I read over the two versions I'd written.

List Poem

We cook chili—
cans of beans
smushed up tomatoes
cans of beans
cut up garlic
cans of beans
chopped up veggies
spices spices.
I can't wait to eat.

Pause for a moment to notice that this unit is not just teaching students about writing poetry. It is teaching them about the process of writing in general. So often, the revision work that children do amounts to adding more information. Here children are learning a far more large-scale and ambitious sort of revision. They're learning too, about the link between reading the work of another author and revising one's own draft.

Conversation Poem

We can do it.
I'll read the recipe.
   I'll open the cans.
Don't forget the garlic.
   Don't forget the beans.
Time for tomatoes.
   You still need more beans.
We're really cooking now.
   We're a team.

"What do you think, class? Which is the structure that conveys the feeling of my brother and me working side by side, sharing the job?"

The children talked for a moment, and then I chimed in. "Let me tell you what I think, and give me a thumbs-up if you were about to say the same thing. For me, I think the conversation poem really brings out how we were taking turns with this job and working together on it. I think the list poem accentuates that we had to add a whole lot of things into the chili. It would be a good structure if I wanted to show how many things go into chili—but not if I am trying to show that my brother and I worked closely."

Debrief. Review the steps you took when trying structures on for size.

"Writers, do you see that when choosing which structure would be best, I thought, 'What do I want readers to feel?' and then I chose the structure that matched what I wanted to say?"

ACTIVE ENGAGEMENT

Recruit children to help a classmate pick a form that conveys his intended meaning.

"Poets, can you help Henry pick a structure for his poem that will fit with what he wants to say? Henry, come on up here and bring your writing." When Henry was seated on a chair at the front of the meeting area, I said, "I already asked Henry what he hopes his reader feels when reading this poem, and he said that he wants readers to feel proud of Tucker! Right, Henry?"

Henry nodded. "I want them to know how smart Tucker is. I want to write about a trick he learned one day that is really cool."

"And you already know that Henry worries that his list poem doesn't give the proud feeling and mood he is after. So, will you think, 'What structure do you think Henry might use for his poem that will fit with what he wants to say?' Will you turn and talk to your partner?"

Give children a minute to chat about this question, but you will probably not be able to let children report back, or your minilesson will last longer than ten minutes. Remember that it is critical to protect time for writing.

116

The children talked, and as they did, I coached into their work. I channeled partners to be specific, to point to lines in the poem, to help each other say more. After a bit, I said, "Poets, give me a thumbs-up if you have some ideas."

"We thought Henry could write a story poem," Silas said. "He could start it, 'One sunny morning Tucker waited for me in the yard.'"

"That beginning does sound like a story. Can you try to convince Henry why the decision to write a story poem might allow him to bring out a proud mood?" I asked.

Silas looked stumped. His partner, Gabriel, jumped in, "'Cause you can show your yard, and you can be teaching Tucker a trick there."

Amira added, "A story poem can tell about a small moment, like about Tucker learning how to roll over."

I said, "So you think a story poem would make it easy to clearly describe one time when Henry felt proud of Tucker. And I bet there are some other structures that would work too, in different ways."

LINK

Reiterate that children have choices as they write today, not just about structure and feeling, but about the ways they put their words together, the sounds they create.

"Poets, as all of you go off to write today, remember that the structure, the kind of poem, you choose can help to get a feeling across to readers. Today you might reread the poems you have written so far in this unit and think, 'Does the structure in which I have written this poem fit with what I am trying to say?'

"Of course, there is a lot of other work you can do today as poets as well. Some of you will be writing brand-new poems. Some of you are working on endings or beginnings for your poems or on your word choices. You've learned a lot these past few weeks, and today you can draw on anything you know how to do.

"When you share later, you're going to walk around and read each others' poems, learning from what you all have done. So as you write today, remember that in just a little while, those poems will be teachers for other poets in this classroom. I cannot wait to see what you teach through your writing."

By letting students know that today's writing will serve to teach other poets in the class, you give them an additional purpose for the day's work. Most will "write up" today, knowing that their poems will be read as inspiration.

A Reminder about Responsive Conferring

AS YOU PREPARE FOR CONFERRING TODAY, remember that you are not only working with students. You are also working on your own conferring. Sometimes you'll find that you feel so pressed for time that you cut short the research part of the conference. Watch yourself as you confer, asking, "Am I listening to each student, each group of students?" If you find that you are teaching the day's minilesson over and over again, this may be a sign that you are approaching each student with a predetermined plan, rather than teaching responsively.

Take time at the beginning of your conferences to ask, "What are you trying as a poet today?" Try to listen in a way that lets your teaching be made-to-order in response to what the youngster says. You can do this even if a student has not yet begun writing for the day.

When I pulled up beside Katharine and asked her what she was working on, she first pulled out her poem "Tornado." (See Figure 13–1.)

After Katharine finished reading, I shook my head and raised my eyebrows, commenting only, "Phew. Tornadoes sure are dangerous. Your poem has a dangerous feeling, a dangerous mood." I wanted her to hear how her poem made me feel. When you give students their words back, they often respond with more words.

"Yeah, I saw a show on tornadoes," Katharine said. "All of the houses were wrecked. It was really sad."

"Katharine, what did you try to do as a poet here?"

"I wanted to show all of the ways the tornado ruins things. It's like a list."

"Absolutely! You know, you did a couple of other interesting things in this poem, too, things you may not even realize. One is that you wrote an *information* poem. This poem gives a reader information about tornadoes. You wrote this as a tornado expert, because you saw a show about the damage that tornadoes do, and you teach your readers about that damage in your poem." Katharine smiled, and I thought about her favorite books in the classroom library—weather books.

"And you do something else here too," I continued. "In this poem, after you teach about a tornado, here—at the end—you tell how you feel about it, that he should be ashamed. It's like a two-part poem. One part information, one part opinion." Katharine nodded excitedly, surprised that she had done something so wise without even realizing it. And I was surprised too, learning a new poetic structure from one of my own students, a new structure we might add to our bulletin board.

MID-WORKSHOP TEACHING   Getting Yourself Out of a Rut

At this point in the unit, you may see that some children are cranking out poem after poem, without stopping to revise any of them. Others may be writing very slowly, as if they are carving in marble. Returning to mentor texts can be one way to help youngsters recognize their own patterns and nudge themselves forward.

"Poets, may I have your attention for a second? There is such a great poetry buzz in the room right now! Here's something I'm noticing, though: some of you are writing so fast that I wonder if you are thinking about what you are writing. All writers get into ruts sometimes. And writing really quickly can be a rut. If you are writing lots of poems really quickly, without thinking deeply, you can change that. You can decide to read a poetry book you love and see if you can find something challenging to try, and then you can work long and hard to do that thing. Or you can study our bulletin board and push yourself to try a new structure or way of using words."

I continued, wanting to solidify this compliment into next steps Katherine would take in her writing. "You know, Katherine, this is a technique you can return to again and again. Sometimes poets are so fascinated by a subject, so interested in a topic that they want to share their new knowledge with others. Remember all those books we read together about simple machines? You might want to go back and reread them, looking at the pictures, reading the text, and see if you find ideas for more information poems. Maybe you will reread some of your favorite weather books, who knows? You might even write a whole collection of nonfiction poems!"

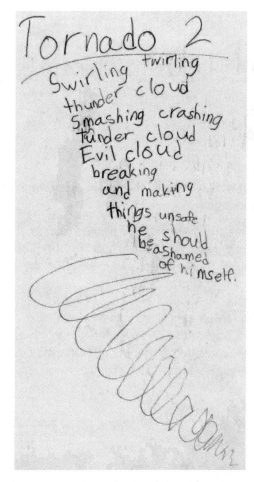

Tornado
by Katharine

Swirling twirling
thunder cloud
smashing crashing
thunder cloud
Evil cloud
breaking
and making
things unsafe
he should
be ashamed
of himself.

FIG. 13–1   Katharine's poem has a dangerous mood.

Learning from Each Other's Work
A Museum Share

Rally your students to share recent work with each other in a museum share. Channel them to walk around, noticing what their fellow poets have done.

"Writers, stay in your seats for now. Instead of sharing with your partners, today you'll have a museum share so that you can see *lots* of different work. Just like you learn about writing from Kristine O'Connell George and Eloise Greenfield, you can learn from each other. Sometimes reading a friend's poem makes you say, 'Oh, I want to try a circle poem, a poem that begins and ends the same way, just like Julia did!'

"Right now, choose the poem that you are proudest of and lay it on the table in front of you. When you've done that, we'll have a museum share. You'll walk around and study each other's poems. As you silently read your friends' poems, see if you can find a poem in a new structure that you want to try. Maybe you'll read a list poem with a great twist ending or a poem with two parts. Can you find places where a poet has made comparisons or used repeating lines or written cool beginnings or endings?

"Read today as if you are going on a scavenger hunt, searching for writing moves that you love, moves that you plan to try in your own work tomorrow."

Playing with Point of View

J OYCE SIDMAN, author of Newbery and Caldecott honor books of poetry, wrote to me once, "When I discover something amazing—like butterfly tongues that curl up into a perfect spiral—I turn to poetry to express my wonder and excitement. In a poem, I can pretend I'm a butterfly. I can imagine what it feels like to have a long, long tongue that unrolls to sip sweet nectar from flowers and then curls up neatly under my chin. If I use really vivid words, I can make other people imagine it, too—just by reading my poem. So my discovery becomes their discovery, my wonder becomes their wonder. Such is the power of poetry."

Pretending to be a butterfly, or role playing, comes naturally to children. They will strut through the house, blankets knotted under their chins like superhero capes. They will wobble around in ladies' high heels or clomp through the house in too-big work boots. In class, too, children often role-play with you, reading picture books in the voices of animals, articles in the voices of historical figures. It can be powerful, therefore, to unleash your students' imaginations in poetry, offering them opportunities to speak in the voices of other people, objects, or animals that they find interesting and inspiring.

This is a lesson in point of view and personification. So far in this bend, children have been exploring different structures of poetry: list poems, conversation poems, story poems. For the most part, they have been writing in their own voices, from their own perspectives. Today they will learn that poets sometimes let the subject of the poem be the speaker. In poetry, everything can come to life, and both moon and pencil can speak.

Inhabiting the thoughts of another person, animal, or even an inanimate object is a valuable exercise in teaching perspective. This "getting inside of a subject" allows a writer to see and understand different aspects of the subject, and "writing as" something will call forth different material than "writing about" something. You can expect, therefore, that this session will enrich children's poetry and also their empathy and their ability to consider multiple perspectives. You might even carry today's lesson with you into later social studies or science units, asking children to once again write from the point of view of someone or something very different from themselves.

IN THIS SESSION, you'll teach students that poets sometimes write from a point of view other than their own.

GETTING READY

✔ "Waiting Room Fish" by Amy Ludwig VanDerwater, written on chart paper (see Teaching)

✔ A classroom or nature object (book, twig) with which you will demonstrate speaking through a mask (see Teaching)

✔ An everyday object full of story, such as a worn down crayon, to inspire children's mask-talk (see Active Engagement)

✔ If you choose, ongoing folders full of poems including some mask or persona poetry (see Link)

Playing with Point of View

CONNECTION

Tell your students that in addition to paying attention to structure, poets pay attention to who's talking—point of view—in their poems.

"Over the past few days, you have been learning many different structures of poems. You know that some poems are shaped like lists, some are like back-and-forth conversations, and some poems tell stories. When you study a poem, there is something else to notice also: who is talking?

"Of course, it is often the poet him- or herself talking. But sometimes, poets will use the voice of somebody else. My nephew Davis, for example, sometimes pretends he knows what his dog is thinking, and sometimes he talks in a funny dog voice, saying, 'Ruff! Let's go for a walk!' or 'Drop your sandwich! I will eat it! Woof!' It's almost like he stops being Davis and puts on a dog mask.

"Poets do the same thing. Sometimes, they stop being themselves and put on a mask, taking on the role of someone or something else. You might remember when Amy did this in "Maples in October." She wrote that poem by wearing the mask of maple trees! Or you might remember how Nathan tried this in his poem "A Good Book to Read" early on in the unit—in that poem, he was wearing a book mask!"

✿ Name the teaching point.

"Today I want to teach you that when experimenting with different kinds of poems, poets sometimes drop their own voice and take on the voice of another person or thing. Instead of writing *about* something, they write *as* that thing. Some call that kind of poetry a *mask poem*, because it is as if the poet is speaking through the mask of someone or something else."

◆ COACHING

Teaching children to be deliberate about noticing whose voice is represented in a piece of writing is big work. It pushes children one step further up the ladder of becoming aware of implicit meanings in texts.

You briefly mentioned point-of-view to your students in the Session 8 Share, but today's lesson will take the concept further—examining how poets can write from a variety of perspectives.

TEACHING

Show the children a mask poem on a chart, highlighting point of view, or how the poem was written through a mask.

"Listen to this poem, 'Waiting Room Fish' by Amy Ludwig VanDerwater, and try to figure out who is talking. Is the poet talking as herself? Is she wearing a mask?" I began reading the poem aloud.

> *Like small*
> *orange birds*
> *we watch you*
> *watch us.*
>
> *We peek between*
> *plastic plants.*
> *We open wide*
> *for food flakes.*
>
> *We wave our tails*
> *inviting you*
> *to join us*
> *for a swim.*

Invite children to share their thinking and ask them to notice how a mask poem is a way to show another point of view.

"I hear many of you saying that the poet is wearing a fish mask—talking in the voice of a goldfish, like the ones in a waiting room aquarium. Notice that by talking in the fish's voice, she forces us to see through the fish's eyes, to consider what the fish must be thinking and feeling.

"I never really thought about what must go on in the mind of a waiting room fish until I read this poem. 'We peek between plastic plants.' What new thing did you realize, considering a fish's point of view? Tell your partner."

I waited thirty seconds, allowing a buzz of conversation between pairs before calling out, "This mask poem has really gotten all of you to see how the fish think, what their point of view is! Share with everyone what you were thinking."

Jace held both hands out, palm up, "I felt like I wanted to swim with them! I didn't ever think that fish watch us. I think it is funny if they want to swim with us."

I nodded, "Poets give us these feelings on purpose. By writing through a mask, a poet can help readers understand different points of view. That is really important stuff!"

You can find many more mask poems in Paul Janeczko's book Dirty Laundry Pile.

Do a quick, oral demonstration of how you might draft a mask poem, using an everyday object in the classroom.

"So if I were to write a mask poem about this clock," I gestured up at the clock on the wall, "I would put on its mask." I paused to stare at the clock for a moment. "And I would make my reader see this clock's point of view." Changing my voice slightly, to imply that I was now talking in the voice of the clock, I thought aloud, as if improvising a poem on the spot, "What would a clock feel like? How can I write from a clock's point of view?" On a chart paper, I began writing.

> I spin my hands
> around my face.
>
> You look at me.
> Everyone looks at me.
>
> I know the time—
> Time to start.
> Time to stop.
> Time for lunch.
> Time for art.
>
> I spin my hands.
> Tick tock.

Debrief what you just did in a way that makes it easy for children to generate mask poems.

"Poets, did you see how I put on the mask of this clock? I used its voice to make the reader consider what this clock probably thinks and feels. I used my poets' eyes to see an ordinary thing, like a clock, in a special way and told the readers its point of view."

ACTIVE ENGAGEMENT

Engage students in partner talk, asking them to imagine the thoughts of an inanimate object and speak as this object might speak.

"So, now that we've had a chance to observe how poets sometimes pretend to become something else by wearing a mask as they write, let's try it out. Let's experiment with pretending to *be* something else, just as poets do." I held up a worn down blue crayon, turning it this way and that in front of the children.

"Look carefully at this old crayon. Study its peeling paper and its flattened tip. Think about its color and what its life has been like so far. Now, poets, please pretend that you *are* this crayon. Talk about your experiences and what you love and do. What are you afraid of? What do you think? Tell your partner about your crayon life. For just a few minutes, speak *as* this crayon."

If you are very slow at writing on chart paper, you can write this on a page tucked under the clip of your clipboard, and the added advantage is that you can actually have the words there already, allowing you to read them as you pretend to invent them. Just keep that clipboard tilted away from view! Later, put your poem on chart paper.

Walking from partnership to partnership, I held the crayon up so the children could see it clearly. I listened as Ramon turned to Rob, "I am a short crayon. I am really scared of the crayon sharpener."

Evette whispered to Nina, "I love to draw sky best! Lots of sky! With birds! Someday I am going to draw blueberries. Maybe today!"

Confirm the talk you heard as students spoke through masks, complimenting their varied and clever mask voices.

"I could hear your crayon voices clearly. Some of you imagined what you would draw next, and some of you told about your hopes and fears. That's just what poets do. They pretend they know what an object would say if it could really talk, and then they write those words as a poem."

LINK

Encourage students to revisit the poems in their folders, noticing the various speakers, before taking up their own writing and revision work for the day.

"Before you begin writing today, read through the poems in your folder, thinking about who the speaker is in the different poems you like best. When you read others' poems, you can learn about how they write mask poems, as different people and objects and animals. Other poems can give you ideas for your own poems."

Encourage children to always remember that poets decide on the point of view of their poems.

"When you write your own poems, ask yourself, 'Who will the speaker be in my poem? Will I wear a mask?' If you want your reader to feel a certain way when reading your poem, pretending to be someone or something else, writing through a mask, may help you bring out the feeling of your poem."

Poems Have Structures

- **Conversation poems** include two voices—"Maples in October"
- **List poems** are lists—"Destiny"
- **Story poems** tell about moments, bit-by-bit—"Fly fishing in the Crystal River"
- **Mask poems** speak in a voice of someone or something else— "Waiting Room Fish"

Stanzas, Hybrid Structures, and Other New Frontiers

TODAY AS YOU CIRCULATE AMONG YOUR STUDENTS, be ready to assess what the students are trying to do and to help them take their next steps. You'll want to make sure that many of them are generating new poems, drawing on today's minilesson, but also on earlier work about generating ideas for poetry.

As you confer about the new drafts that students produce, you'll find that students' increasing abilities as poets will lead them toward new challenges. For example, presumably many of them will be writing with a level of volume that you didn't see earlier. If this is the case, their longer poems will benefit from being divided into parts. This can

MID-WORKSHOP TEACHING   Introducing a New Point of View: Poems of Address

"Writers, can I stop you for a minute? I want to share something new and interesting with you about point of view, something that Nina noticed in her folder of poems just now." I waited as the children looked up from their poems.

"Nina was reading Lilian Moore's poem 'Go Wind,' one of our old favorites, noticing how Lilian wrote the lines of her poem. Nina noticed Lilian did not write a mask poem. She is not pretending to *be* the wind. Instead she is speaking *to* the wind. Listen."

> Go wind, blow.
> Push wind, swoosh.
> Shake things
> Take things
> Make things
> fly.

"Can you hear how Lilian talks to the wind? She's pretending that the wind can hear her. Well, after Nina read Lilian's poem, she jotted, 'Lilian talks to the wind but the wind is not a person.' Nina is right. The wind is not a person, but poets pretend. And you know what? Nina pretends too. She decided to try this kind of poem herself, speaking *to* something else, something that's not a person.

"Lilian has written a poem to the wind. Nina has written a poem to a tree. Poems that talk to subjects—to trees and wind and people and anything—are called *poems of address*. Imagine yourself talking to something or someone that doesn't talk

back. Imagine the possibilities! You could write a poem of address to your pillow, your pet, your friend, the sidewalk, the bus, the sky." I let my voice trail off.

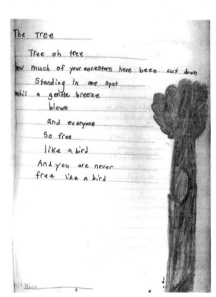

FIG. 14–1   Nina speaks to a tree in her poem.

The Tree
by Nina

Tree oh tree
How much of your ancestors have
    been cut down
Standing in one spot
Until a gentle breeze
blows
and everyone
so free
like a bird
And you are never
Free like a bird

be the perfect time to help your students understand stanzas. Like paragraphs, stanzas separate parts of a poem—one voice from another, a shift in setting, a change in action or tone. Teach stanza secrets such as if a poem has several stanzas, often each of those stanzas has same number of lines. If poems have stanzas, there is sometimes something in each stanza that repeats. A new stanza usually signals that something new will be coming. Of course, you can also teach children that they can glean stanza tips from studying mentor poems with this lens.

As you confer about children's work today, you may find that writing in new points of view leads some children to write riddle poems. If you see children doing this, make

them famous. Declare that they have invented yet another structure for poetry. Help them search for and study mentor texts, and set them up to create their own bulletin board display featuring riddle poems.

Then, too, as children demonstrate all they know about structures, you may see some of them begin to make poems that combine two structures. A child may say to you, "My poem is a list poem and it's a mask poem too. It's my cat telling a list of all her favorite kinds of birds to eat." Celebrate these innovations.

Poems Have Structures

- **Conversation poems** include two voices—"Maples in October"
- **List poems** are lists—"Destiny"
- **Story poems** tell about moments, bit-by-bit—"Fly fishing in the Crystal River"
- **Mask poems** speak in a voice of someone or something else—"Waiting Room Fish"
- **Poems of address** speak to a specific person thing—"Go Wind"

Poets Try New Things and They Collect Ideas for New Poems from Their Everyday Lives

Close the session by reading aloud a poem by a child who tried something new, who stretched beyond today's minilesson, and whose poem offers something new.

"Poets, earlier we talked about how poets can imagine that they are anything in the world—a dog, a ballerina, a train—and write from that point of view. And reading your poems, I can see that many of you experimented with point of view today, pretending to be all sorts of things. Reed wrote from many points of view today. Listen!" (See Figure 14–2.)

"Kara wrote a mask poem today, and it's a riddle poem too because instead of writing a title, she wrote the answer at the bottom. I am going to read Kara's poem to you, and I want you to listen very carefully. See if you can figure out who the speaker is in this poem. See if you can figure out the riddle of Kara's mask poem." (See Figure 14–3.)

Maanav called out, "I know! It's Earth!" And as he said this, many other children nodded, whispering under their breaths triumphantly, "I knew it!"

"Which lines in Kara's poem helped you figure out the riddle?" And they answered, "The 'spinning' line." "The 'blue and green' line." "The 'planet friends' lines." "Kara used such clear lines that you knew just what the poem was about. And it was clever of her to write a mask poem as a riddle poem too."

Remind students that they can use their poets' eyes and imaginations all through the day, that poets have ideas all day long and save them for writing time.

"I am going to add today's new kinds of poems to our bulletin board—mask poems and riddle poems too. And when you are home riding your bike later today or snuggled in your favorite chair, pay close attention. If you suddenly think, 'Oh, my bike loves going down hills!' or 'This chair holds me on its lap,' keep those thoughts in your pocket. Any time you wonder or imagine what other things or animals or people are thinking, you have the beginning of a mask poem."

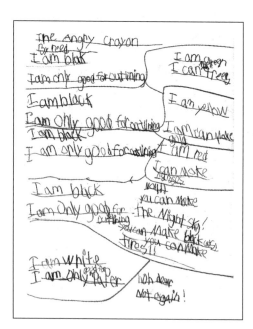

FIG. 14–2   Reed writes from many points of view.

The Angry Crayon
by Reed

I am black.
I am only good for outlining.

    I am green.
    I can make trees!

I am black.
I am only good for outlining.

    I am yellow.
    I can make gold

I am black.
I am only good for outlining.

    I am red.
    I can make red roses

I am black.
I am only good for outlining.

    NO!!!
    You make the night sky!
    You can make black cats!
    You can make tires!!

I am white.
I am only good for paper.

    Oh dear.
    Not again!

128

Build excitement for the upcoming celebration.

"Tomorrow you will begin rereading through all of your poems, getting ready to choose and revise and edit for the celebration that's coming up. You know so many ways to use your poets' eyes now, and you know so many ways to revise. I can hardly wait for the celebration!"

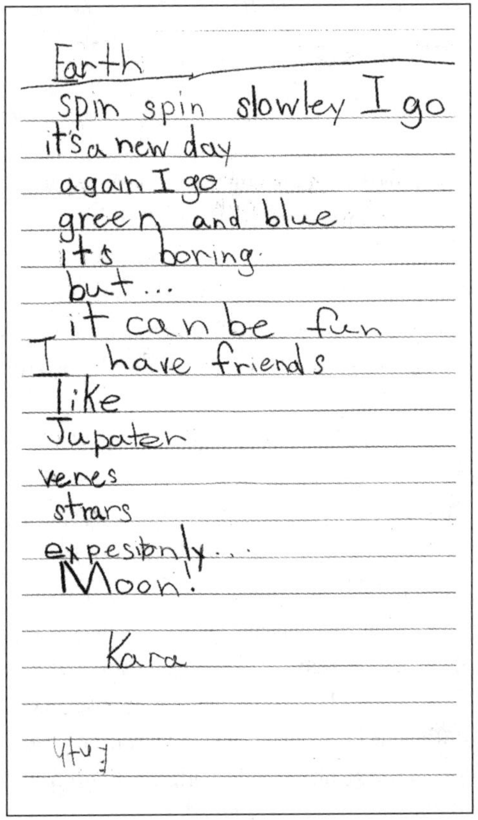
Earth
spin spin slowley I go
it's a new day
again I go
green and blue
its boring
but...
it can be fun
I have friends
like
Jupater
venes
strars
expesibnly...
Moon!
Kara

FIG. 14–3 Kara's mask poem that is also a riddle

Spin spin slowly I go
it's a new day
again I go
green and blue
it's boring
but . . .
it can be fun
I have friends
like
Jupiter
Venus
stars
especially . . .
Moon!

(Earth)

Poems Have Structures

- **Conversation poems** include two voices—"Maples in October"
- **List poems** are lists—"Destiny"
- **Story poems** tell about moments, bit-by-bit—"Fly fishing in the Crystal River"
- **Mask poems** speak in a voice of someone or something else—"Waiting Room Fish"
- **Poems of address** speak to a specific person or thing—"Go Wind"
- **Riddle poems** reveal hints about their subject directly to the reader

Session 15

Revising Poems
Replacing Feeling Words with Word Pictures

IN THIS SESSION, you'll teach students that poets revise by replacing vague feeling words with images that show rather than tell.

GETTING READY

✓ A teacher-written poem about a class experience, written in a way that leaves room for "show, not tell," revision (see Teaching)

YOUR CHILDREN will have been revising throughout the unit, and now as the unit draws toward a close, you will want to create extra enthusiasm for revision. Be sure that you approach revision with a joyful spirit. Think of revision as playful exploration. Encourage your children to carry their poems with them throughout the day, rereading them often in case they get a new idea for how to improve them. Eve Merriam, one of the most widely anthologized poets in the United States explains, "Sometimes I've spent weeks looking for precisely the right word. It's like having a tiny marble in your pocket; you can feel it. Sometimes you find a word and say, 'No, I don't think this is precisely it...' Then you discard it, and take another and another until you get it right." This sense of revision as play is one you will want to embrace today; writers enjoy imagining ways to improve their writing. Many writers consider revision their favorite part of writing, and you will want to celebrate this process, noticing what a big difference small changes can make and noticing, too, that sometimes one gets an idea for a whole new and much better draft.

Your children will probably have a bunch of poems that they wrote at the very start of the unit—poems they may not have reread for a long time. The distance will have given them perspective, and also their skills will be better now, so they'll be able to revise by bringing those skills to bear. Many writers revise after their work has been out of sight for a week or longer. As Kristine O'Connell George, author of *Old Elm Speaks*, says, "Know how there are all those different plays in football and how a team practices them repeatedly? I do something like that when I play with an idea for a poem: I experiment with different forms and take different points of view. Try the poem with rhyme or without rhyme. Then, a poem in progress spends time 'resting' inside a dark desk drawer. When I take the poem out, perhaps months later, I can often see ways to make it better."

While there are endless ways to revise a poem, in this minilesson, you'll highlight just one particularly important sort of revision (reserving others for your conferring). In today's session, you'll reiterate the "show, not tell," strategy that you have taught before, helping children understand that this applies equally, if not more, to poetry. You will help your children paint pictures with words, substituting those word pictures for lines of telling, such as "I felt mad."

Revising Poems
Replacing Feeling Words with Word Pictures

CONNECTION

Explain that poets often let their writing sit for a while before revising it, to see it with fresh eyes.

"Your folders are now full of poems," I held my flattened hands a few inches apart to indicate this fullness, "and you may have many poems that you haven't read in a long time." Children nodded, and I went on. "Poets do this. They let their writing sit for a while, and then they come back to it later. Kristine, who wrote 'Fly Fishing in Crystal River,' says that she keeps her writing in a dark drawer and sometimes doesn't reread or revise it for months! Coming back to your writing later helps you see the things you want to change and add because the poem feels almost new to you, and your eyes are fresh."

❖ **Name the teaching point.**

"Today I want to teach you that when poets revise, they look at a poem with brand-new eyes, asking, 'How can I make this work even better?' One way to do this is to look for opportunities to show, not tell."

TEACHING

Explain that the entire purpose of poetry is to show, not tell, and provide a few quick examples.

"I can hear you thinking, 'What? Show, not tell? We *already* know about that!' You're right. You already know what show, not tell, means because it is something you did when you were writing Small Moment stories. But poets, in particular, are *masters* at showing, not telling. That's the entire purpose of poetry.

"A poem won't say, 'It began raining.' Instead, a poem will go, 'Plop! Fell the First Drop! Umbrellas unfurled like daisies!' And a poem won't say, 'The cat was angry.' It will probably say, 'Hiss, scratch, spit! Bottlebrush tail! Run for your life!' The best poems show us actual pictures that let us almost see and feel what is happening."

◆ COACHING

If your connection has nothing especially fun or important or lively in it—that's okay. Just keep it brief and to the point.

I contrasted a dull voice for "telling" about rain with a much brighter voice for "showing" the scene of the first few drops.

Share one of your poems that you have picked for revision.

"Today I want to start by reading one of my poems to you. Will you help me think about whether there might be part of the poem where I tell, instead of showing? I could then maybe try to fix up those parts. Listen up." I read the poem aloud, emphasizing lines that I hoped children would see needed to be revised.

Behind My Desk

My students give me pictures
to hang behind my desk.
When I look at them
I feel so happy.
I see a crayon cat
curled on a chair
sleeping in yellow sun.
I see a red butterfly
and big planes flying.
These pictures make me glad.

"This poem shows your artwork. I can almost see the cat and the sun and the butterfly and the airplanes." I pointed to the different lines of the poem, ones that clearly showed rather than told. I then contrasted these with the lines that told feelings.

"But I'm thinking there were parts of the poem where I'm still telling, not showing. Let's see," I said, giving children time to assess this with me. I pointed to "I feel so happy" in the fourth line. "This is true. I *do* feel happy when I look at your artwork, but I'm just *telling* the reader this. I am not *showing* the reader my happiness."

Demonstrate the process of revising your poem so that it now shows something that was being told before.

"Watch as I take this line, 'I feel so happy,' and try to paint a picture that really shows my happiness." I closed my eyes for a minute, thinking aloud to myself.

"Hmm, what does it look like when I feel happy? What would someone see if they saw me becoming happy?" I placed my hands on both cheeks and smiled, "Well, I do this! I hold my cheeks and grin." I looked back at the poem, back at the children, still holding my cheeks, grinning wildly.

As always, you will want to emphasize that writers choose to revise writing that is already good, already worthy, already loved. Poets choose to publish poems with the most potential, and it is an honor for a poem to be selected for revision.

It is true that quick tips such as "show, not tell" sometimes lose their meaning and fall to cliché. You will need to support these tips with plenty of ready examples and demonstrations, in small groups and conferences, until children internalize the true concept of showing, not telling.

"Let's see if this new line will work in my poem." I read the poem out loud, listening to and evaluating the new line.

Behind My Desk

My students give me pictures
to hang behind my desk.
When I look at them
My serious face becomes a grin.
I see a crayon cat
curled on a chair
sleeping in yellow sun.
I see a red butterfly
and big planes flying.
These pictures make me glad.

"Yes! A serious face becoming a grin shows a picture of a changing mood. An artist could draw that. I will keep this revision."

ACTIVE ENGAGEMENT

Invite the children to imagine a new last line for this poem, replacing feeling words with actions or a word picture that an artist could draw.

"Now let's look at the last line of this poem: 'These pictures make me glad.' Again, it is true, but do you think I am just telling this? Would it be hard to draw this line? (That's a hint that I've told it, not shown it.) Will you act out what you would actually do if pictures made you glad, and then think how you could change the line to make it better?" After a minute, I asked children to talk to their partners.

After a bit, I said, "Poets, I heard so many good ways of showing that I feel so glad. Henry thought of the line, 'I trace the pictures with my fingers.' And you know, I do that! Henry's line shows me doing something with my body. He shows my fingers tracing your artwork. I can picture it, and it gives me a glad feeling."

You may want to reread sessions from Lessons from the Masters *in which you taught students to show not tell.*

LINK

Send kids off to study their own poems, looking for lines to revise.

"When you get to work today, I know you'll be revising poems for our celebration. One way you might revise will be to reread your poem to see if you can find a line where you told, instead of showed, things. Paint a picture in your mind of what an artist might draw to show that line of the poem, and then go ahead and write a new line! When we share in a bit, I will ask for some of you to read us your lines and then to let us hear how you turned them into pictures that show instead of tell the important feelings in your poems."

Supporting End-of-Unit Revision

B Y TODAY, your students will have a whole repertoire of possible structures that they can choose to write in, and of course, they'll also have all the qualities of good poetry that they've learned across the unit. They shouldn't have any shortage of options for ways to work! Given that the unit will be approaching its conclusion, you may decide to especially prioritize helping students revise. That doesn't mean this will be the only focus of your small-group work and your conferring, because you always need to be ready to respond to the needs you see in your kids, but you might take a few minutes prior to the workshop to imagine possible ways to support revision today.

It helps to consider some of the challenges you're apt to encounter as you channel kids toward revision so that you can think in advance about ways you might handle those challenges. You may find that a few of your kids surprise you by using revision as a time to make their free verse poems into rhyming ditties. Adding rhyme wouldn't, in and of itself, be a problem, but sometimes when youngsters decide to try rhyming, they sacrifice meaning. For example, I was recently conferring with Christina, who'd taken a poem that originally contained lines such as "I am learning to speak cat. I whisper purrs in bed," and rewritten it so that the entire poem sounded more like this: "My cat likes to sleep. My cat likes to purr. My cat likes to climb. She does not stir."

You'll want to honor students' attempts at rhyming, but you'll show them that a poem's meaning is primary. In this case, I wanted Christina to realize that forcing rhymes may have actually weakened her poem. "Sometimes, an important message does not fit into any ready rhyme," I told her. "And that's okay. Try reading your poem aloud *before* and *after* you make a revision and listen to the words. Which words are the strongest? Which words bring out strong images or feelings? Hang on to those words, even if you can't find a word to rhyme with them." You'll want to teach children to revise in ways that strengthen, rather than weaken, their writing. *(continues)*

MID-WORKSHOP TEACHING   Sketching First to Show Feelings

"Writers, you are finding so many different ways to tackle problems that you encounter as you work on your poems. Klara, for example, was having a hard time coming up with the exactly right words to capture the feeling that she felt when she got a hamster for her birthday, so she first just turned over her paper and started listing possible ways to capture that feeling in words. She wrote phrases like 'I was really surprised' and 'I couldn't believe it.' That wasn't really working for her, so she invented a different way to tackle her problem. This time she sketched. And you know what? That helped. She ended up finding that half way through her sketch, words came to her mind."

I held up Klara's paper for everyone to see, walking around the classroom as I explained Klara's new technique. "Look. Right here, where Klara had written 'I was super excited' you can see a tiny little picture. See? In this wee drawing, Klara has her mouth open wide, and her eyebrows are sticking up into the middle of her forehead."

I looked up to see Klara making this same surprised face for the class and continued, "Now Klara's poem line reads, 'My eyebrows jumped off my face!' instead of 'I was super excited.' The readers of Klara's poem will know that she was excited because of the word picture she wrote about her eyebrows. Sketching helped Klara make a picture with words. Maybe this strategy of making tiny sketches will help some of you show your feelings too.

"My bigger point is that when you find yourself not sure how to do something, when you want to throw your hands up in the air and cry, 'Help me, help me,' remember that you can help yourself. You can do as Klara did and invent your own solutions to problems. You may not brainstorm ways to say something or sketch as a way to rehearse for writing, but you can come up with solutions that fit your problem and that work for you."

Some children will work on finishing touches to their poems—especially endings and titles. When I pulled up alongside Carolyn, she announced that her poem needed an ending:

Stuffed Animals

Look on my bed!
Soft brown bear
One-eyed cat
Fluffy blue bunny
Little old dog
Snake from the fair
Snuggly raccoon

"I can just picture all those stuffed animals, their different colors, sitting right on your bed. It makes sense that you wrote a list poem like Zoë did, going down the page with a different animal on each line. So what are you thinking for the ending?"

Carolyn answered, "I don't know. I might write, 'I love my stuffed animals.'"

Children often default to clichéd lines such as "I love my . . . " at the endings of poems in the same way that they default to drawing rainbows and smiley faces in the early days of kindergarten. I wanted her to know that because poems are short and concentrated bits of language and because poets work tirelessly to avoid clichés, it is common for poets to generate lots of possible endings before choosing one. So I told her that poets think of a bunch of possible endings and then choose the best and told her there is one question that can really help a poet get a good ending. I paused for dramatic effect.

"This is the question. Why is this topic very important to you? What matters here?"

Carolyn squinted her eyes. "They're my friends in the nighttime."

"Yes." I kept listening, "What else?"

"They've known me for a really long time, 'cause I got the bear when I was two. It is kind of like, sort of like, they understand all about me!"

I stopped Carolyn. "Carolyn, do you hear what you just said? You just said some true things about your stuffed animals, and each thing you said could be an ending to your poem." I then said back a cleaned-up, sparser version of what she had said to me.

They're my nighttime friends. They've known me forever. They understand everything.

"What beautiful lines. You are giving your reader a big feeling for how much you love those sweet animals without saying, 'I love them because . . . ' Lots of kids love their stuffed animals, but you found a way to tell people about the particular kind of love that you feel toward yours."

Then, wanting her to extract some transferable tips from the conference, I said, "Remember, Carolyn, whenever you write a line of a poem, you can always think about a few different choices. That will be especially important to do when you write beginnings and endings because they are so important. Sometimes a phrase like 'I love . . . ' will show up in your mind first, but instead of just writing that down, ask yourself, 'Why is this very important to me?' The answer to that question will help you know what to write."

Poets Elicit Strong Feelings by Painting Pictures in Readers' Minds

Celebrate the way that one child's poem elicits strong feelings through clear images.

"Writers, Mason is going to read his poem. As he reads, listen for the places where Mason's writing gives you a strong feeling. After you listen to the poem, I will ask you to share the feeling you got and also which lines gave you that feeling. Ready?" I waited until the room grew completely silent before beginning. (See Figure 15–1.)

Invite children to share the feelings they got from the poem and which images brought those feelings out.

"Now turn to your partner, and tell what feeling Mason's poem gave you. Which words or lines in the poem made you feel this feeling? Which images?"

I listened in as Maddie said to her partner, "It's a scary poem."

I voiced over to the class. "Be sure you point to the specific parts of the poem that gave you the feeling."

Maddie added, "He uses a lot of scary words, like *sharp, pointed,* and *watch out*!"

"Yeah," added Davis, "He says 'Watch out' two times!"

Remind children that it is their words that make readers see and feel.

"Anytime you write, you will want to remember this. You, the poet, are the one who makes a reader feel. You can make your readers feel scared, like Mason did, or surprised, like Klara did in her poem about getting a hamster for her birthday. You paint the pictures, and readers see and feel those pictures inside their minds. This is the power of writing."

Looks like an Eagle
It looks like an eagle.
It eats dead animals
It is a bird of prey.

sharp claws
big eyes
Pointed beak
Awsome flier

If youre a small critter
watch out!
watch out!

by Mason

Looks like an Eagle
by Mason

It looks like an eagle.
It eats dead animals.
It is a bird of prey.

sharp claws
big eyes
pointed beak
Awesome flier

If you're a small critter
Watch out!
Watch out!

FIG. 15–1   Mason's poem elicits strong feelings.

Editing Poems
Reading Aloud to Find Trouble Spots

IN THIS SESSION, you'll teach students that poets often read their poems aloud to find trouble spots.

GETTING READY

✔ A teacher-written poem that can be edited for sound (see Teaching and Active Engagement

✔ "Language Conventions" portion of the Opinion Writing Checklist, Grade 2, students used in Session 5 (see Link)

P OET J. PATRICK LEWIS SAYS, "I tell kids endlessly, always read poetry out loud. You want your ears to have as much fun as your mouth is having." This session is the last before your students celebrate their poems. It will focus not only on editing, but also on helping students reread their writing aloud for sound and balance, making changes accordingly.

While children will edit today for all of the usual things, using their now-familiar editing checklists, your emphasis will be on editing through *listening*. More than any other genre, poetry is written for the ear, and today's lesson will teach your students that professional writers read their work aloud, over and over, considering every punctuation mark, every line break. Oscar Wilde is credited with having said, "I was working on the proof of one of my poems all the morning, and took out a comma. In the afternoon I put it back again." While you should not expect your students to go to this extreme, you will teach them that each mark, each word counts in a poem.

Writing poetry is similar to playing music. Violinists develop a musical ear by listening to virtuosos, and so do poets. By listening to all of the poems you have read aloud this year and in the context of this unit, your class knows the sounds of poetry. In describing her process, author Mem Fox explains, "When I write, I hear." This is true of all writers, and today you will teach your students to listen to the words, silences, and music of their own poems. Like a musician knows when a song is in the proper key or when the timing is off, so too should poets ask themselves, "Does this sound right?"

Earlier in this unit, your students edited their poems paying special attention to spelling, and today you will expect your class to reread to check for spelling errors. Those are hard to hear. But before they read with their eyes, you will invite them to read with their ears, hearing the music and silence of their poems and asking, "Does this sound right? How could I make this sound even better?"

Editing Poems
Reading Aloud to Find Trouble Spots

CONNECTION

Rally students' energy for this final editing session before celebrating their poetry. Explain that poets edit with their ears as well as their eyes.

"Our poetry celebration is just around the corner. I keep thinking about how lucky our visitors will be to get to hear and see your poems. You're probably expecting that today's work will be about getting your poems as ready as they can be to share with your audience. We've talked before about spelling and how punctuation changes a poem and how poems look different on the page than prose, and you worked on editing those things. But you also know that poets care about the *sound* of their poems, and today you will edit your poems the way poets do.

Of course, all the emphasis on repeated read-alouds will also pay off for students' development of fluency. There is no grade level where expectations for fluency skyrocket more than in second grade, so it is appropriate that this unit places such an emphasis on reading aloud.

"Did you know that in addition to reading poems with their eyes, poets read with their ears?" Smiling at their bemused looks, I continued. "Just as drivers listen to their cars for trouble spots and rattles, asking, 'Is this car ready for the road?' writers listen for trouble spots, asking, 'Is this poem ready for a celebration?' Poets often read their own poems out loud, listening for rattles. Amy Ludwig VanDerwater, for example, even makes recordings of her poems and listens to herself reading her poems as a way to listen for the rattles and creaks that signal that something needs to be fixed."

❖ Name the teaching point.

"Today I want to teach you that one way poets edit their poems is by reading them aloud, listening for places where the words or lines do not sound right. Then, they go back to these places and write new lines, reading aloud, listening, and always asking, 'Does this sound right?'"

TEACHING

Demonstrate reading the first stanza of a poem out loud, listening for and rewriting lines that do not sound right.

"Listen carefully as I show you how I reread the first stanza of my poem, 'Spider,' listening for a line that may not sound right." I read the poem aloud, making sure to read aloud the lengths of the line breaks.

Spider

Spider draws a web
all the way across the window in my room.
a circle web around.
She is an artist.
My window
is her frame.

I looked at the poem and cocked my head, asking myself aloud, "Does this sound right?" My students didn't answer, curious to hear what I thought. "When I read this stanza out loud just now, I noticed that the second line sounded so much longer than all of the other lines. It didn't seem to fit the rest of the poem. We know that sometimes a poet might write one line especially short or long for a particular reason, but there isn't a reason here. It's just long, and hearing my voice read it aloud helped me to see that doesn't really sound good. I'm going to change it."

Thinking a few new line possibilities aloud—"in my window," "right outside," "a silver window web"—I crossed out line two, changing it to "in my window." "Let me read it again." I read the poem again, loud enough for children to hear, but clearly for my own ears. "Yes, that's much better. Reading my poem out loud helped me hear that trouble spot and know where to make a change."

ACTIVE ENGAGEMENT

Set students up to work on reading the second stanza of the poem aloud, listening for a place that does not sound right.

"Now you try it! I have the second stanza of 'Spider' here too." I gestured to the second stanza of my poem. "And it's your turn to read this second stanza out loud under your own breath, listening for a part that doesn't sound right to you." I looked at the children whose attention was already on the poem, "Ready? Read aloud and think, 'What doesn't sound right to me?'"

Spider eats flies
lots and lots
of disgusting
f flies.
e is a chef.
indow
itchen
ng.

You may want to have children spread out around the room since their work will require that they whisper their poems into the air, listening to their own voices. During the share, they will have an opportunity to be out-loud readers for each other.

139

Invite the children to share words or lines from the poem that did not sound right to them.

After listening for a few minutes, I asked the children to share what they were thinking. "Which places did your listening ears tell you didn't sound right?"

Klara pointed to the third line, "I don't think that the word 'disgusting' sounds right. It's supposed to be a pretty poem. Maybe it could say 'tasty' instead."

"I don't like the last line, where it says 'for cooking.' That feels like extra stuff. All kitchens are for cooking. You should just cross out that line."

Say the children's words back to them, complimenting their careful out-loud reading and recommendations.

"Writers, you heard many things that didn't sound right when you read this stanza. Some of you noticed words that didn't match the meaning, like 'disgusting,' some of you commented that 'lots and lots' sounded a little boring, and some of you talked about how my ending, 'for cooking,' felt like extra words. These are all things that poets listen for when they read their own poems out loud too!"

LINK

Send students off to edit their own writing first by reading aloud, then by using their editing checklists.

"Now, writers, today when you go off to get your poems ready to share and celebrate, remember that one way poets edit is to read *with their ears*. Reading aloud can help you find problem spots that you might not have noticed otherwise. You might want to find a good working place where you can hear your own voice reading your poem. Then, read your poem out loud, listening for any trouble spots, any places where it sounds like you need a new line or a shorter line or an extra word added in or taken out or changed. Of course, some parts of editing you'll definitely need your eyes for, so don't forget that you can use the "Language Conventions" part of our writing checklist to check for capital letters, commas, apostrophes, and spelling as well."

Some of your students may not find any lines of this poem to be problematic, but if this example simply copied the trouble in the first stanza (line length), children would likely gravitate toward this same issue. By offering a stanza that some children might find acceptable, you push them to find something that "doesn't sound right." They need to stretch.

Your students may try to edit today by listening to the sounds of their poems and may not actually improve the quality very much at all. It is important for you to remember that children must try a technique over and over before they achieve mastery over it. So do not fret if a few of today's poems do not actually improve from a poem-quality standpoint. Your greater goal is to teach your children to become writers who, like so many of their favorite poets, read and listen to their work aloud.

Supporting Students' Editing Work

YOUR STUDENTS' WORK TODAY is likely to fall into two parts. At first, they will be curled up with their folders in various corners of the room, reading their poems aloud and listening for what doesn't sound right. During this time, you might sit down next to individual children, asking them to share where their reading aloud is leading them to fix a word or line. Expect that some students will not have found any such places, and in these cases, offer to read a child's poem aloud to her, suggesting it might help to hear if you make any errors in reading. Remember, though, that the point of today's minilesson is for students to hear the "not right" places themselves, and your goal is to help them listen to their own work. Compliment your students' careful reading aloud, reminding them that reading aloud, listening to their writing, will help tune their ears to the music of poetry.

The second part of today's work will find children working with the editing checklists, now reading their poems for capital letters, commas, apostrophes, and spelling. Editing poetry is as much about making choices as it is about correctness, and this is the time to bring up questions of whether children are choosing to capitalize every line as some poets do or only lines that begin a new sentence. Will they use punctuation in a special way?

Spelling is not as open to interpretation as punctuation, even in poetry, and you may notice that some children continue to breeze right by misspelled words. You can remind ⁺tudents that they can always make themselves "Give It a Shot!" charts (see Session ⁺o help find the correct spelling.

As you meet with groups today, stress the importance of reading aloud well, in a strong clear voice and with meaning. Your celebration is tomorrow, and how students read poems will be almost as important as what poems students read. Encourage children to read with voices that match meaning, reminding them that their voices are a part of a poem's music. You might read one of your own poems aloud to demonstrate how your voice carries the rhythm and mood of your poem.

MID-WORKSHOP TEACHING   **Placing Capitals**

"Poets, eyes up here for a moment. We have learned to capitalize the beginnings of sentences, holidays, names of people and places, and days of the week. But poets often use capital letters differently. Just now, Francesca told me that she is going to capitalize every line of her list poem because every line tells a new idea. And you know what?" I made the thumbs-up sign. "Francesca told me that she got this idea from rereading Zoë's poem 'Inside My Heart.' That's what all poets do. They read others poets' poems to get ideas for their own poems. So today as you edit for capitals, remember that looking at the mentor poems in your folder might help you make your editing decisions. Poets make decisions; they don't just stick capitals anyplace. Ask Francesca."

Reading Our Writing Aloud as an Editing Strategy

Rally partners to take turns reading each other's work aloud so that each poet can have a turn listening for any stumbles on the part of the reader.

"Poets, today you read your own poems aloud, listening for the lines that didn't sound right. You have become editing readers for yourselves, finding places to add a word or change a line break. It can be difficult to hear the places where your own poems are hard to read, though. This is why it can help a writer to hear a partner read his or her poem aloud, to just listen for places where a reader might have trouble reading the poem.

"Partner 1, would you please give one of your poems to Partner 2? Then Partner 2, you will read Partner 1's poem out loud just as it is written on the page. Your reading will help Partner 1 know if there might be some tricky spots for readers, spots that need to be edited. Partner 1, you listen for places where your partner struggles with reading your poem, places where Partner 2 makes a mistake or stumbles. Those might be spots where you need to change something. After you have a moment to mark the places you want to think about changing, I will give Partner 1 a turn to read Partner 2's poem, listening for places that might need a little more editing.

"Listening to someone else read your work aloud is a great technique that you can use anytime you think your writing is finished. Sometimes hearing another person read your words will help you hear what to fix."

AFTER THE CELEBRATION

Following the celebration, you might tell students that you wouldn't dream of packing away all these poems into file folders never to be thought of again. Back in the classroom, they can illustrate their poems, create and discuss word clouds, and comment on one another's poems. You may want to give them a moment to reflect on the unit, now that the frenzy and excitement of publishing and celebrating are behind them. You might be surprised to know how they respond to questions such as "What do you know about poetry that you didn't know before?" "How are you strong as a poet?" "What was hard for you about poetry?" or "How would you explain poetry to a Martian?" You might also consider collecting all of the students' poems into a classroom anthology, naming it together, and giving each child a copy to take home and cherish.

We hope it's been rewarding, and that you saw and created things you never thought you could!

Congratulations to you and the second-grade poets!

Lucy, Stephanie, and Amy

Invite the children to share words or lines from the poem that did not sound right to them.

After listening for a few minutes, I asked the children to share what they were thinking. "Which places did your listening ears tell you didn't sound right?"

Klara pointed to the third line, "I don't think that the word 'disgusting' sounds right. It's supposed to be a pretty poem. Maybe it could say 'tasty' instead."

"I don't like the last line, where it says 'for cooking.' That feels like extra stuff. All kitchens are for cooking. You should just cross out that line."

Say the children's words back to them, complimenting their careful out-loud reading and recommendations.

"Writers, you heard many things that didn't sound right when you read this stanza. Some of you noticed words that didn't match the meaning, like 'disgusting,' some of you commented that 'lots and lots' sounded a little boring, and some of you talked about how my ending, 'for cooking,' felt like extra words. These are all things that poets listen for when they read their own poems out loud too!"

LINK

Send students off to edit their own writing first by reading aloud, then by using their editing checklists.

"Now, writers, today when you go off to get your poems ready to share and celebrate, remember that one way poets edit is to read *with their ears*. Reading aloud can help you find problem spots that you might not have noticed otherwise. You might want to find a good working place where you can hear your own voice reading your poem. Then, read your poem out loud, listening for any trouble spots, any places where it sounds like you need a new line or a shorter line or an extra word added in or taken out or changed. Of course, some parts of editing you'll definitely need your eyes for, so don't forget that you can use the "Language Conventions" part of our writing checklist to check for capital letters, commas, apostrophes, and spelling as well."

Some of your students may not find any lines of this poem to be problematic, but if this example simply copied the trouble in the first stanza (line length), children would likely gravitate toward this same issue. By offering a stanza that some children might find acceptable, you push them to find something that "doesn't sound right." They need to stretch.

Your students may try to edit today by listening to the sounds of their poems and may not actually improve the quality very much at all. It is important for you to remember that children must try a technique over and over before they achieve mastery over it. So do not fret if a few of today's poems do not actually improve from a poem-quality standpoint. Your greater goal is to teach your children to become writers who, like so many of their favorite poets, read and listen to their work aloud.

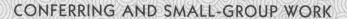
Supporting Students' Editing Work

YOUR STUDENTS' WORK TODAY is likely to fall into two parts. At first, they will be curled up with their folders in various corners of the room, reading their poems aloud and listening for what doesn't sound right. During this time, you might sit down next to individual children, asking them to share where their reading aloud is leading them to fix a word or line. Expect that some students will not have found any such places, and in these cases, offer to read a child's poem aloud to her, suggesting it might help to hear if you make any errors in reading. Remember, though, that the point of today's minilesson is for students to hear the "not right" places themselves, and your goal is to help them listen to their own work. Compliment your students' careful reading aloud, reminding them that reading aloud, listening to their writing, will help tune their ears to the music of poetry.

The second part of today's work will find children working with the editing checklists, now reading their poems for capital letters, commas, apostrophes, and spelling. Editing poetry is as much about making choices as it is about correctness, and this is the time to bring up questions of whether children are choosing to capitalize every line as some poets do or only lines that begin a new sentence. Will they use punctuation in a special way?

Spelling is not as open to interpretation as punctuation, even in poetry, and you may notice that some children continue to breeze right by misspelled words. You can remind students that they can always make themselves "Give It a Shot!" charts (see Session 5) to help find the correct spelling.

As you meet with groups today, stress the importance of reading aloud well, in a strong clear voice and with meaning. Your celebration is tomorrow, and how students read poems will be almost as important as what poems students read. Encourage children to read with voices that match meaning, reminding them that their voices are a part of a poem's music. You might read one of your own poems aloud to demonstrate how your voice carries the rhythm and mood of your poem.

MID-WORKSHOP TEACHING   Placing Capitals

"Poets, eyes up here for a moment. We have learned to capitalize the beginnings of sentences, holidays, names of people and places, and days of the week. But poets often use capital letters differently. Just now, Francesca told me that she is going to capitalize every line of her list poem because every line tells a new idea. And you know what?" I made the thumbs-up sign. "Francesca told me that she got this idea from rereading Zoë's poem 'Inside My Heart.' That's what all poets do. They read others poets' poems to get ideas for their own poems. So today as you edit for capitals, remember that looking at the mentor poems in your folder might help you make your editing decisions. Poets make decisions; they don't just stick capitals anyplace. Ask Francesca."

Reading Our Writing Aloud as an Editing Strategy

Rally partners to take turns reading each other's work aloud so that each poet can have a turn listening for any stumbles on the part of the reader.

"Poets, today you read your own poems aloud, listening for the lines that didn't sound right. You have become editing readers for yourselves, finding places to add a word or change a line break. It can be difficult to hear the places where your own poems are hard to read, though. This is why it can help a writer to hear a partner read his or her poem aloud, to just listen for places where a reader might have trouble reading the poem.

"Partner 1, would you please give one of your poems to Partner 2? Then Partner 2, you will read Partner 1's poem out loud just as it is written on the page. Your reading will help Partner 1 know if there might be some tricky spots for readers, spots that need to be edited. Partner 1, you listen for places where your partner struggles with reading your poem, places where Partner 2 makes a mistake or stumbles. Those might be spots where you need to change something. After you have a moment to mark the places you want to think about changing, I will give Partner 1 a turn to read Partner 2's poem, listening for places that might need a little more editing.

"Listening to someone else read your work aloud is a great technique that you can use anytime you think your writing is finished. Sometimes hearing another person read your words will help you hear what to fix."

Presenting Poems to the World
An Author's Celebration

ear Teachers,

When we work with adults and older children, we often ask them to make timelines of themselves as writers: "Let's make timelines of our lives as writers. Put the moments that have mattered most into your timeline." Often, before we talk about our writing histories, we ask people to reflect on their timelines: "What have the turning points been in your writing life?" Time and again, people respond by telling about a time long, long ago, when their words were published. "I really felt like an author," they confide.

As teachers, we need to move heaven and earth to be sure every child knows what it is to be a published author. It's for this reason that you've gone to great lengths all year to celebrate your children's writing. Now, as this unit on poetry comes to an end, you'll want to design a finale. Invite your children to join in the fun. "What should we do?" you'll ask.

We've seen classrooms organize "coffee houses" that feature poetry readings. We've seen children use xylophones and recorders (and accompanying hand gestures) to set poems to music. We've seen classrooms decide to give poetry away, creating literary gifts that include framed poems and recorded readings of poems. We've seen anthologies of all sorts and sizes.

In this celebration, you'll help children make their poems public by posting them in the community and reading them to various audiences. This can be as elaborate or simple an adventure as you choose. You might confine your posting to the school building itself, or you might choose to go farther afield.

We'll offer suggestions for publishing work electronically, to connect with a larger audience. Using technology can have a way of taking over a unit and become an exercise in "doing cool stuff" rather than in using the resource purposefully. You'll want to keep this celebration first and foremost as a way to make a human connection. The emphasis in this book remains on children's literal participation in their physical community. That said, the use of technology to create and share visual and auditory records of poems redefines what we consider our audience to be and widens the circle of influence children's poetry can have in the world.

PREPARING FOR THE CELEBRATION

The celebration we describe here has two components: performing the poems aloud and posting copies of them in the community. You have asked children to practice reading their poems aloud many times during this unit, and you have focused on the importance of music for weeks. Because of this, the specific preparation for performing, or reading with feeling, for the celebration will need to be only minimal. You may want to have kids mark up their poems, using any notation they need to remember any decisions they made with respect to vocalization.

To prepare for posting copies of the poems around the neighborhood, you will want to have already asked students to consider fitting places to hang up their poems. You will want to confirm that hanging poems is indeed permitted in these places and find alternatives with students' input, if possible, as well as make sure a trek to each place is feasible. You'll need enough small copies of their work and any materials required to hang the poems in the chosen locations. A nice souvenir of the day is a small map of the neighborhood with the poem-hanging places noted, with the poet's name next to a dot on the map. If you choose to divide your class into small groups for the posting part of this celebration, you will want to have arranged this strategically beforehand as well.

In addition to our literal poem-posting, our technology teacher helped us create an interactive map of sorts, using Glogster. We created a web page with photographs of all the places we hung poems. Each photograph could be clicked on, and an image of the poem appeared, accompanied by the voice of the child reading it. Children also used Voicethread to compile a DVD slideshow of their poems and illustrations, again accompanied by their own readings of the poems (this could have been created in Microsoft PowerPoint or Keynote, as well, and presented on a large screen to families). Some children explored using Wordle or Tagxedo to create word clouds of their poems, which they hung up with their poems and used to create cards for friends and family. This changed the poems, but in a way that created interesting conversation about a poem's big feelings and small moments or images. (See Figures 17–1 and 17–2.) We kept our use of these digital resources to a small number so we could give kids time to explore the possibilities offered by each, rather than be dazzled by a million different ways to use the Internet and computers.

CELEBRATION

As your guests arrive and settle in, give each child and guest a copy of the map or itinerary of poetry stops. Take the children to the first place and have the student perform and post that poem while everyone listens. As mentioned earlier, it may be more feasible to do this in small groups. Decide what makes the most sense for your class and your school. Continue through the rest of the itinerary, giving each poet a turn to

FIG. 17–1   Klara's "Moon" poem word cloud

FIG. 17–2   Nina's "Tree" poem word cloud

read and maybe even reflect on their learning in this unit if time permits. You might even want to pull out all of the stops and get ice cream! Afterward, don't forget to post copies of all the poems on a classroom bulletin board or tuck them into a beautiful class poem book. Poems such as Francesca's "The Evening" need to live in your classroom all year long, reminding your students of poetry's power. (See Figure 17–3.)

As our celebration began, children and their families met at the school for a celebration breakfast and then headed into the world, poems in hand. Abuzz with excitement, the class headed to a kiosk in a nearby park, where Daniel posted his poem. The group gathered close, pulling in curious onlookers, and Daniel read his poem aloud (see Figure 17–4).

We continued with the trip, performing poems and leaving them behind. Tired and a little hungry, we sat on the grass outside the school while a parent ran off to get some popsicles. When we returned to the classroom, it was time to pack up and go home, but not before we read one last poem hanging near the art supplies, a poem of many voices. A handful of children read Reed's poem together. (See Figure 17–5.)

The Evening
By: Francesca

I look upon
this evening
the grass

tickling my feet.
I look up
see the clouds

thrown carelessly
across the sky.

People picnicking,
like flowers,
dots of color.

Everything
has a tint
of pale blue,
like a painting,
an artist,
trying to make,
it all match,
just right.

FIG. 17–3   Francesca's writing reminds us of poetry's power.

Trees

Did you know that squirrels
  plant more trees than people?
They sometimes forget where they
  buried their food.
Digging.
Down in the ground
Deeper
And faster
He drops his food
Under the dirt.
A few days later
He forgets
A little sun
A little water
And BOOM!
A tree

FIG. 17–4   Daniel

The Angry Crayon
by Reed

I am black.
I'm only good for outlining.

  I am green.
  I can make trees!

I am black.
I'm only good for outlining.

  I am yellow.
  I can make gold!

I am black.
I'm only good for outlining.

  I am red.
  I can make red roses!

I am black.
I'm only good for outlining.

  NO!!!
  You make the night sky.
  You can make black cats.
  You can make tires.

I am white.
I'm only good for paper.

  Oh dear.
  Not again!

FIG. 17–5   Reed's poem of many voices